"When I die, my epitaph or whatever you call those signs on gravestones is going to read: 'I joked about every prominent man of my time, but I never met a man I dident like! I am so proud of that I can hardly wait to die so it can be carved. And when you come to my grave you will find me sitting there, proudly reading it."

WILL ROGERS COOKBOOK

1879-1979

A COLLECTION OF
RECIPES FROM
CELEBRITIES, POLITICAL
FIGURES, AND "JUST
PLAIN FOLKS"
COMMEMORATING
THE 100TH BIRTHDAY
OF WILL ROGERS

Will Rogers
COOKBOOK

---

with the sayings of Will Rogers

Will Rogers Cooperative Association
of Will Rogers State Historic Park
California

Palisades Publishers —— Pacific Palisades, CA 90272

Photographs

WILL ROGERS COOKBOOK

Copyright © 1979 Will Rogers Cooperative Association
A non-profit organization of docents who are dedicated to keeping the memory of Will Rogers alive for all America to enjoy.

Library of Congress Catalog Card No. 79-88115

International Standard Book No. 0-913530-19-0

Printed in the United States of America

Credits
Art—Don Raymond
Pictures—from the archives of Will Rogers State Historic Park, Pacific Palisades, California.
Quotes—Will's sayings throughout this book are used with permission of Dr. Reba M. Collins, curator of Will Rogers Memorial, Claremore, Oklahoma.

DEDICATED TO THE MEMORY
OF WILL ROGERS

"When you have helped to raise the standard of cooking, you have helped to raise the only thing in the world that really matters anyhow. We only have one or two wars a lifetime, but we have three meals a day."

Will Rogers

I wish to express my appreciation to the Will Rogers Cooperative Association members who have volunteered great amounts of time and energy in creating this cookbook.

Cooperative Associations are created for the purposes of supplementing the interpretive programs in units of the park system. These associations are non-profit organizations authorized to generate income to be used in implementing a complete, professional interpretive program for the park visitor.

Cooperative Associations are also encouraged to sponsor Docent programs. The Will Rogers Association has a very active docent operation, a docent being defined as a non-paid interpretive guide.

This Cookbook is an excellent example of volunteer effort accomplishing an interpretive project, at the same time generating income that will assist in other interpretive endeavors involving Will Rogers the "man" and the environs of his "Santa Monica Ranch."

M. Carl Wilson
Manager,
Will Rogers State Historic Park
Pacific Palisades, California

ACKNOWLEDGMENTS

There has been a warm and generous response to our requests for help with this book—from the Will Rogers family, from governors of 50 states and from officials from every unit of government. Friends of Will Rogers from stage, screen, and the media all wanted to be part of the book as well as those good folks who spend so many hours keeping the Will Rogers State Historic Park in safe keeping for us all to enjoy. Friends in the community of Pacific Palisades who are proud to have the memory of Will so close also submitted their culinary master-pieces. We appreciate those who shared their own favorites and hope the reader will enjoy this rich collection of delectable dishes.

We wish to acknowledge the assistance of Dr. Reba N. Collins, curator of the Will Rogers Memorial in Claremore, Oklahoma and especially for the permission given us to use the Will Rogers quota-tions throughout the book.

Carl Wilson, Area Manager of Will Rogers State Park has given us great support for this book. Elyse Keane, Harriet Axelrad and Jan Jones assisted me in the testing of the recipes and Harriet Axelrad has given me many kind words of encouragement while getting these pages to press. Donna Howard was a great help in typing recipes.

Finally, I want to thank my best friend, my husband Don, for his patience and help. His art work of western artifacts has also added to the theme of the book.

Thanks to all who were so generous with their prize recipes—for a book to honor a great American, Will Rogers.

Donna Raymond, Editor

WILL ROGERS

A "ropin' fool" they called him,
This man one can't forget.
He walked with Kings and Princes
And liked each man he met.

He read the daily paper,
He said that's all he knew,
His homespun witty comments
Helped hone the public's view.

His gracious way of living
Included many guests
Who listened to his wisdom
And chuckled at his jests.

If you should come to visit,
To picnic, or to hike,
You'll find his ranch house open,
And that is what he'd like.

Though he's not there to greet you,
Just think that though he flew
To unknown lands far distant,
A welcome waits for you.

Harriet L. Axelrad
Will Rogers Docent

BIOGRAPHY—WILL ROGERS
NOVEMBER 4, 1879
AUGUST 15, 1935

"There was something neighborly about him," Mrs. Rogers wrote in loving remembrances of Will, "something that made you feel as though you had always known him."

It was this something that secured a permanent place for Will Rogers in the hearts of the American people. To them he was more than an actor, humorist, or journalist. He was their spokesman, the voice of the 1920s and 1930s, the conscience of America.

He won the love and respect of his countrymen with his great humanity and his jovial but pointed commentaries on the political abuses and social inequities in the national affairs of his time.

The sound wisdom behind his barbs, his genial nature and the sparkling freshness of his humor endeared him even to those who were his favorite targets. To be the subject of Will's satire was a sort of status symbol. His shrewd wit was completely without bitterness and was amicably aimed at the foibles and follies of bigwigs and to protest whatever encroached upon the rights and welfare of the people. In so doing he made the whole world laugh.

Will was born William Penn Adair Rogers on November 4, 1879, in Indian Territory, now the State of Oklahoma. Both parents were of partial American Indian ancestry through the Cherokees. Scotch-Irish forebears had married into the tribe on the father's side, and Dutch and Welsh on the mother's.

Will was the youngest of four surviving children in a family of eight. His father, Clement Vann Rogers, was an enterprising, ambitious and independently wealthy cattleman and rancher. Rogers County was named for Clem Rogers and was the district he represented in the constitutional convention which resulted in statehood for Oklahoma.

Will's mother, nee Mary America Schrimsher, bestowed upon her only surviving son a gentle love and a marvelous sense of humor, two gifts which remained with him throughout his lifetime. Her death when he was ten years old was a traumatic experience for the young boy.

Young Will was given every advantage in order that he might be encouraged to follow in his father's footsteps. But he had one great love—the lariat, which, along with his sense of humor, brought the wrath of his teachers down upon him, but which eventually led to fame, fortune and world acclaim.

Will's career began in Wild West shows. His cowboy roping and riding acts carried him around the world and finally to New York City and the theatrical circuits of the early 1900s. By 1915 he had reached the top in vaudeville. His roping skill and incisive wit made him the featured attraction at the famous Palace Theater in New York City. Shortly after, he became a part of the Midnight Frolic on the roof of the New Amsterdam Theater and later joined the Follies of Florenz Ziegfeld, Jr. From there he moved upward into silent films and on to Hollywood, California in 1919.

Will's experience in silent films was disappointing and without any lasting success, as was a temporary venture he made into producing silents on his own. He found it financially necessary in 1921 to return for a time to the Follies.

At this time he began to develop and use his talents as a banquet speaker, lecturer, newspaper columnist and later as a radio commentator. Through these media, especially his newspaper columns, more than through his films, Americans learned to love him, and his name became a household word.

Will's weekly column first appeared in the New York Times in December, 1922, and was soon syndicated. Four years later his Daily Telegram, a commentary on world affairs, was initiated and syndicated as "Will Rogers Says . . ." It eventually became a feature in more than 500 newspapers in the U.S.

Film stardom came to Will with the advent of talking pictures. His first "talkie" was made in 1929, when he was almost 50 years old, and by 1933 he and Marie Dressler were the top box-office attractions. A year later he was at the top by himself, and at the time of his death, he was still the leading attraction along with Shirley Temple.

Of his marriage to Betty Blake in 1908, Will said, "The day I roped Betty I did the star performance of my life." Mrs. Rogers was the guiding factor and stabilizing influence in Will's life and career. She recognized his genius and unselfishly devoted her time and efforts, her life, in support of him. She was his companion and mentor during their life together. Three sons and a daughter were born to them. The youngest child, Freddie, died in 1920 in Hollywood.

After Freddie's death and until 1927, the Rogers lived in Beverly Hills. In 1928 they moved to their Santa Monica ranch which was Will's home for the last seven years of his life.

On August 15, 1935, a tragic airplane crash in Alaska took the life of Will and of his friend, the famous pilot, Wiley Post. Will's untimely death at the peak of his career confirmed his status as a national folk hero. His own words, spoken many years before, simplistic as they were, seemed strangely prophetic: "This thing of being a hero, about the main thing to it is to know when to die."

Will was the living embodiment of the philosophy of individual freedom, social equality and the natural goodness of man. He lived this philosophy in his associations with others, both the humble and the great. He was a friend of the poor, of kings and princes, men of letters, the great leaders of the world. Four American presidents welcomed him to the White House during their respective administrations. They were Warren Harding, Calvin Coolidge, Herbert Hoover and Franklin Roosevelt. For them he was America's Ambassador of good will.

His ranch home in Pacific Palisades, now Will Rogers State Historic Park, is a repository of memorabilia of his life. They are reminders of his human relationships, his pride in his Cherokee background, his homely philosophy and the simple virtues that shaped his character—kindness, honesty, humor, generosity and love.

FOREWORD

I am very pleased that the Docents at the Will Rogers State Park are putting out this cook book, for one of the things I inherited from my father was a very good appetite and another was a total lack of culinary talent.

Since Dad came from Oklahoma and grew up on country cooking his favorite dishes were plain and simple. He sure liked a mess of hot biscuits covered with cream gravy. Chili was high on his list of favorite foods. But I think that a big bowl of white, navy beans cooked with ham hocks and served real soupy would be his first choice.

I can remember many nights he and I sat in the big room. Lilly, the cook, would bring in a crock. It must have held a little better than half a gallon, filled with those soupy beans and big chunks of ham floating around, and a platter piled high with fresh corn bread. We would smother the corn bread with beans and sit there and eat and talk until that old crock was empty.

Now I sure wish I could give you the recipe for this mighty fine dish, but like Dad I'm more of an eater than a cooker. I can, however, give you my one and only recipe which I must admit I got from Dad. I can guarantee that it is fool proof. All you have to do is marry a good cook.

James B. Rogers

ON COOKBOOKS AND COOKING
by Will Rogers

from the 1931 introduction to the
Beverly Hills Women's Club Cookbook

The Ladies (apparently) of the Beverly Hills Women's Club (yes, they got one), I don't belong to it, but it's here performing the usual function of all organized men or Women's Clubs, that is, trying to find something to do. Well these Ladies decided to get out a Cook Book. Now I don't know of a better place for a Cook Book to originate than in our City of Beverly Hills. For here the cooking is done by Cooks and not by Amateurs. Course there are a few local Wives that for pastime, or for the news reel Photographer, will dawn a Gingham creation, and detour to the kitchen, but this reign of indigestion in the family is only slight. The culinary Art returns to normal, and the Wife returns to her pursuit of love and happiness generally within a day's time.

So in that way we get good Cooking. You see this is an age of specialization. It's awful hard to be a good Cook and a loving helpmate. You can do the two, but one is apt to detract, one is bound to sooner or later suffer. There is bound to crop up a tinge of Ptomaine in the kitchen, or a slacking of helpmating in the rest of the home.

So we go out and get the best Cooks we can (well, we also go out and get the best Wives we can). But it's not wives we are discussing now, it's good Cooking. Course we got some mighty fine recipes in here by some of our most distinguished, and also lovely wives, but they only drew up the Blue Prints or ground plan. It's like an Architect. He tells you how to build a house, but did you ever see one he built for himself?

Now I don't mean by this that our Ladies can't cook as good as any other Wives anywhere else, for they can. But it's better cooking than that is what we are after, and that's our excuse for distributing this Pamphlet. Pretty near any woman can cook ordinary, (not only can but do,) but it's Super Cooking we are diagnosing for you in this Gem of Appetite. What am I doing in the book? I have the right of any wronged stomach to be here, I am here to assist my fellow man from having to eat some of the things that I have had to eat during the past. When you have helped to raise the standard of cooking, you have helped to raise the only thing in the world that really matters anyhow. We only have one or two Wars a lifetime, but we have three meals a day. There is nothing in the world that we do as much of as we do eating. Even sleeping don't start to compare with it. There is only one recipe for sound sleeping, that's a comfortable seat and a poor picture, or a political speech.

Now the little Almanac of calories that follows will give you the ingredients of about all the different combinations that have been worked out with food as a background. Some of these were stumbled onto accidentally by reaching on the wrong shelf. A great many of the best ones in here were not premeditated. Cooking is a good deal like Jokes . . . there are only seven original ones, and it takes a lot of scrambling 'em up to get something that sounds or tastes different. To be a good cook you got to be either naturally an experimenter, or just clumsy.

The French have a reputation for good cooking when it's only a reputation for Camaflouge that they deserve. They can hide more ordinary food under some kind of sauce, and by the time you dig through the sauce, your palate is in no mood to recognize the original Goat meat hiding under the sauce. They can put a liquid overcoat, and non-pronounceable name, on a slice of horse meat and have an American wondering if it's breast of veal, or Angel food cake. It's that gravy those Frogs pour on there that does the dirty work. They are just naturally sauce hounds. And over there the Government decorates men for dishing up food in such a way that no one knows what it is. Cooking is not a necessity with them, it's an Art. And that's what these good Women of this Club (well, I guess we got maby some good Women that are not in the Club), but it's the ones in the Club that I am telling you of now. I am just going to tell you "how to read the book" to get the most out of it. This is not an introduction; it's another recipe.

First you get hungry. This is no book for a satisfied stomach. The hungrier you get the better the book will appear. Naturally as you get hungry you start imagining, imagining what you would love to have to eat. When you get your mind set on just about what you would rather have than anything else in the World to eat why you turn to that particular page of the book where that particular type of food is advertised and there will be the prescription for that very dish that you have been craving to devour. Any kind of ration you can think of, some member of this Club thought of it before you did, cause we got plenty time out here to think, and you will find a plot of it right in this directory. Now I don't know how it's going to taste to you, for no two people have the same taste, and besides I don't know how you are going to mix it, no two people mix things the same. Tea cups are not always the same size, different hens lay different eggs, naturally. What you would call a "heaping teaspoon full" some stingy person might take for a saucer full. But if you follow the general directions in here you will land somewhere in the neighborhood of what our good Lady intended. If you haven't got all the ingredients, don't let that worry you. For in all these we have naturally allowed some leeway, and you can use something else. You won't get exactly what she was driving at, but you may get an improvement. Now take bread. I think it was H. G. Wells or maybe it was Brisbane who said, "Bread is the staff of life." Some of it is, and some is just an obituary notice. Now in here we tell you where to buy good bread. Study this little catalogue and meet your husband every week end when he drops in. Meet him with one of these prepared little antidotes, try 'em on him and then study him. There is an old Long Beach Proverb that reads, "The way to a man's stomach is through his eyes." Now we have some beautiful dishes in here, in fact some of 'em are better if you just make 'em and look at 'em, they are too good to eat. As I said before, eating is the biggest thing we have. You can talk disarmament, Ramsey Mac-

Donald, Hoover's fishing, and all that, but it's eating that's keeping us here. So if these good Ladies can help the world to better food, they will have performed a true service to everybody and a giant blow against indigestion.

Will Rogers.

Reprinted from the Beverly Hills Women's club cookbook printed in 1931. Permission to use this introduction was given by Mrs. Herbert Olson, President.

CONTENTS

Main Dishes

Will Rogers.

Corned Beef and Cabbage a la Dinty Moore

Will Rogers, Jr.

Dad used to love to go to Dinty Moore's in New York for Corned Beef and Cabbage, and so did Florenz Ziegfeld. Mr. Ziegfeld had Dinty Moore send it to Palm Beach (by train in those days) for a dinner party he was having for 30 people.

Dinty Moore's was a favorite hangout of theatre people. It had spanking white tablecloths, mirrors above the dado rail and sawdust on the floor.

One of the Chefs from Dinty Moore's came up to cook at the Ziegfeld camp in Quebec, Canada. This is the way he made Corned Beef and Cabbage.

4 lb. piece of well-corned beef (brisket or round)
If only mildly corned add:
1 garlic clove
several whole pepper corns
bay leaf

Cover with boiling water and simmer 4 hours until a fork can penetrate to the center.

Wash and drain 1 or 2 heads firm cabbage cut in wedges; simmer on top of corned beef the last 15 minutes of cooking.

Serve with boiled white potatoes.

(About Food) *"Know what's in it before you eat it."*

Joel McCrea Recipe

I'm not much of a cook so my recipe won't amount to much. However anything to do with Will Rogers touches my heart—so here goes—

1 cup (large) beans
1 cup stewed tomatoes
1 sliced onion
3 eggs—plus seasoning
Serve hot with sour dough toast.

Regards,
Joel McCrea

Note: Joel McCrea is the National Chairman of the Will Rogers Centennial Committee.

"My Stew—Your Ragout"

The ingredients include:
2 lbs. cubed venison
4 tblspns. bacon grease
1/2 cup burgundy wine
2 cups water
1 8-oz. can tomato sauce
2 cups stewed tomatoes
3 chopped carrots
1/2 cup chopped yellow onions
3 tblspns. flour
1 dash paprika
1 dash curry powder
1 dash garlic salt
3 stalks chopped celery
4 large potatoes, quartered

Now, when I say a dash of garlic salt, or any other condiment, I mean just enough to give your dish a hint of that flavor. It doesn't take too much curry for me. It might take two tablespoons for you, but I doubt it.

Put the grease, onions and flour in a large cooking pot over medium heat. When the grease bubbles, add the meat. As the meat browns, add the salt and paprika. When the venison is browned add the other ingredients. Cook for two to three hours over just enough heat to keep the ingredients bubbling.

This is one big pot that must be watched. The mixture should be stirred frequently to keep the stew from burning, and you may find it necessary to add additional water to the mixture as it cooks. When the meat is cooked tender you may wish to add some thickening (a cup of water and two or three tablespoons of corn starch) to the stew.

My Stew—Your Ragout goes just great with a fruit salad, some french bread (for sopping up gravy) and your favorite beverage.

You can use just about any wild game meat for this recipe—I prefer venison. It's exceedingly important to me to carve as much fat as possible off venison, or any other wild game meat, before cooking. The fat gives the meat a taste I can do without. You may wish to change the recipe a tad to fit your taste buds. Be my guest. Anyone who follows every recipe to the letter has never lived a full life, in my cooking world.

Sincerely,

Gary E. Quinliven
Information Officer
Dept. of Parks and Recreation

Chef Quin

"We are living in an age of publicity. It used to be only saloons and circuses that wanted their name in the paper, but now it's corporations, churches, preachers, scientists, colleges and cemeteries."

Family Pie

One handful of forgiveness,
One heaping cupful of love,
A full pound of unselfishness.
Mix together smoothly with complete Faith in God.
Add two tablespoons of wisdom,
One teaspoon of good nature for flavor,
Then sprinkle gently with thoughtfulness
and you'll have a never-fail Family Pie.

My name is Montie Montana, and one of the richest treasures of my lifetime, was knowing Will Rogers. Even today, after all of these years, I can set back and recount every single meeting, and each conversation I ever had with Will Rogers. He was that kind of man—Unforgettable! It is with great pride that I add my name to this book.

P.S. I'm not much of a "cook"—but I believe anyone that follows this recipe, will find it a "never-fail."

Montie Montana

Elephant Stew

1 elephant (medium size)
2 rabbits (optional)
lots of brown gravy
salt & pepper to taste

Cut elephant into bite size pieces. This will take about two months. Reserve the trunk—you will need something to store the pieces in.

Add enough brown gravy to cover. Cook over kerosene fire for about four weeks at 465 degrees.

This will serve about 3,800 people. If more are expected, two rabbits may be added. Do this only if necessary as most people do not like to find hare in the stew.

REALLY GREAT FOR A CROWD

Don Towne—
Docent, Will Rogers State Park

Paella Amigos

Serves 6

Lobster, cherrystone clams, mussels, olive oil, chicken, veal, lean pork, garlic, saffron, asparagus tips (fresh or canned), onion, salt, pepper, ripe tomatoes, rice, sweet red pepper, frozen peas, frozen artichoke hearts, crab meat, pimiento.

SEAFOOD
Remove meat from: a 1-1/2 pound lobster. Scrub 6 cherrystone clams and 6 mussels. Pick over: 1/2 pound crabmeat.

MEAT
Cut into parts: 1 frying chicken. Dice 1/4 pound veal and 1/4 pound lean pork.

PAELLA
1. In a heavy deep skillet heat 1/4 cup olive oil.
2. Add chicken, veal and pork. Cook until chicken pieces are browned on all sides.
3. Add: 1 clove garlic, minced, and 1 onion, finely chopped. Cook, stirring, until onion is transparent.
4. Add: 2 teaspoons salt, 1/4 teaspoon freshly ground pepper, and 2 ripe tomatoes (1 pound), peeled and chopped. Cover and cook for 10 minutes longer.
5. Add: 2 cups rice and 4 cups water. Stir to combine.
6. Add: 1 sweet red pepper, chopped, 1 package frozen peas and 1 package frozen artichoke hearts. Cover and cook over low heat for about 20 minutes.
7. Mash in mortar: 1 clove garlic and 1 teaspoon saffron and add to paella. With large spoon turn rice from top to bottom to mix well.
8. Add the crabmeat and the lobster meat, cover, and cook for 10 to 15 minutes longer.

GARNISH: Meanwhile, put mussels and clams in a heavy pot with 1/2 cup water. Cover and bring to a lively boil over high heat. Cook for 2 minutes, or until shells open. Cook 12 asparagus tips until tender in boiling salted water (or heat canned asparagus).

PRESENTATION

Arrange rice mixture in shallow paella dish or large shallow casserole. Place open mussels and clams in their shells on top of rice and garnish with the asparagus tips and strips of pimento.

Governor Jerry Brown

State of California

"California always did have one custom that they took serious . . . that was in calling everything a 'ranch'. Everything big enough to spread a double mattress on is called a 'ranch.' "

Healthy Pizza

1-1/2 cup warm water (hot to hands)
1-1/2 T yeast
1 T honey
Stir and put on pilot light or in a warm place until foamy. While yeast is developing combine in another bowl:
3 bell peppers, chopped
1-2 onions, chopped
3-4 cloves garlic, chopped or pressed
8 or so mushrooms, chopped
1 12 oz. can tomato paste
1 12 oz. can water
Lots of Italian Herb Seasoning. Add extra oregano.
Salt to taste

Back to the crust:
To foamy yeast mixture add and stir
1 t salt
1 T oil
Add flour (whole wheat pastry combined with some unbleached white flour is a good combination)
Add enough to make a soft kneadable dough.
Knead dough lightly, divide in 2 parts. Place on lightly oiled cookie sheets. Roll out with a floured rolling pin, or stretch with hands. (Pick the dough up and let gravity stretch it until the pan is covered with a thin layer of dough.)

Put tomato mixture on top of raw dough layer.
Slice thinly or grate cheese.
1 lb. Precious Mozzarella Cheese
Spread it evenly over the top of both pizzas. Add vegatables, salami pepperoni, or other ingredients to taste.
Bake in oven at 425 degrees till cheese lightly browned 12-15 minutes.

Debbie Brodrick
State Park Ranger CPI

Veal or Turkey Parmegiana

2 pounds veal cutlets, about 1/2 inch thick, cut into six pieces, or
3 Turkeyloins, cut in half across the width
Pound with mallet or edge of saucer.

Breading mixture:
1/2 c fine, dry bread crumbs
1/2 c parmesan cheese
Combine bread crumbs and Parmesan cheese. Set aside.

Mix together:
3 eggs, well beaten
1 T water
1 t salt
1/2 t pepper

Heat 1/3 cup vegetable oil in a large heavy skillet. Dip cutlets into
egg mixture, then in crumb mixture. Now redip them again. Brown
cutlets in skillet; remove cutlet from pan, and use a paper towel to
remove any excess oil. Return cutlets to the pan.
Pour tomato sauce over cutlets
2 8 oz. cans tomato sauce with mushrooms, plus a handful of
mushrooms
6 slices mozzarella cheese, top cutlets with cheese
Simmer covered 10 minutes for veal.
Simmer covered 20 minutes for turkey.
Makes 6 servings.

Wes and Donna Howard
State Park Ranger

*"The Lord so constituted everybody that no matter what color you are you
require about the same amount of nourishment."*

Baked Snapper with Crab Meat, Mousseline Sauce

8 servings

Ingredients:
2 four-pound red snappers, cleaned and fileted (4 pieces)
1 pound lump crab meat
Salt
Pepper
3 teaspoons dried dill weed (or 3 tablespoons fresh chopped dills)
3 tablespoons lemon juice
12 tablespoons butter, melted (1-1/2 bars)

Preheat oven to 425 degrees

Instructions:
Place two fileted pieces of 2 four-pound red snappers in shallow oiled baking dish. Pick over 1 pound lump crab meat to remove cartilage and toss it gently with salt and pepper to taste, 3 teaspoons dried dill weed (or 3 tablespoons of freshly chopped dills), 3 tablespoons of lemon juice and 6 tablespoons of melted butter. Spread 1/2 crab meat mixture over pieces of snapper already in dish and cover with two remaining pieces. Secure with skewers. Pour remaining melted butter (6 tablespoons) over fish and bake for about 35 to 40 minutes in preheated 425 degree oven or until fish flakes easily. Arrange on warm serving platter. Remove skewers and garnish platter with crisp watercress or parsley as described. Serve with mousseline sauce.

MOUSSELINE SAUCE

Ingredients:
4 egg yolks
2 tablespoons lemon juice
1/2 pound butter, melted (2 bars)
Salt
Pepper
1/2 cup heavy cream, whipped

Instructions:

Place 4 egg yolks in blender; add 2 tablespoons of lemon juice and blend quickly. Set blender to slow speed and gradually add 1/2 pound of melted butter. Blend for 2 to 3 minutes or until sauce thickens. Salt and pepper to taste. Whip 1/2 cup heavy cream until stiff and fold into sauce.

Thank you very much for your recent letter. I'm delighted that you have given me an opportunity to contribute to the celebration of Will Roger's one hundredth birthday.

As you requested, I'm enclosing one of my family's favorite recipes. I hope that the readership of your cookbook will enjoy Baked Snapper with Crabmeat and Mousseline Sauce as much as we do.

Sincerely,

John D. Rockefeller IV
State of West Virginia

"Had breakfast this morning with John D. Rockefeller, for which I received a fine breakfast and a brand new dime. Went out with him and watched him play eight holes of golf, for which I received another dime.
Made 20 cents clear. Received more jokes from him than I gave, as he is certainly keen and has a great sense of humor.
Had a very pleasant morning and would have stayed longer, but he run out of dimes. I am trying to get him to come to California for his second hundred years.
Who else will give me a dime to eat with them?"

Beef Tenderloin

2 Beef Tenderloin Strips Each Weighing 3-1/2 lbs. Tie Together
Soy Sauce
Worcestershire Sauce
Salt, Garlic Salt
Fresh Ground Pepper
Bacon

Sprinkle beef tenderloin all over with soy sauce and Worcestershire sauce, garlic, regular salt, and fresh ground pepper. On top, crisscross with bacon. Secure with toothpicks. Let stand at room temperature for 3 hours.

Bake the beef tenderloin for 45 minutes at 475 degrees or for 30 minutes at 500 degrees. Let stand 5 minutes, then slice. Serve the beef tenderloin with warm Bearnaise sauce.

BERNAISE SAUCE

1/2 cup dairy sour cream
1/2 cup mayonnaise
2 tablespoons terragon vinegar
1/2 teaspoon salt
1 teaspoon terragon leaves
1/2 teaspoon dried shredded green onion

Combine the above ingredients and cover. Refrigerate. Before serving, warm gently. This sauce can be served cold when the tenderloin is served cold.

Serves 10 to 12.

Thanks so much for your recent letter requesting a recipe representative of the State of Kansas. I am more than happy to fulfill this request and I feel compelled to brag a bit on the recipes I am sending.

On February 11, 1975, President Ford visited our capitol city of Topeka and my wife, Olivia, prepared the meal for the President and nine midwestern

Governors. All in attendance were very complimentary about the food and Olivia's meal really was a huge success.

Thank you for your interest in the State of Kansas.

Very sincerely,

Robert F. Bennett
Governor of Kansas

Mousse of Sole with Hollandaise

Put in the blender in the following order:
5 files of sole (cut into pieces). Filets must be fresh, not frozen
1 cup light cream
5 eggs
4 egg whites
2 tbsp. melted butter
salt and pepper

Blend mixture for 3 minutes or until smooth. Combine with 1 cup light cream and transfer to a casserole. Put casserole in pan of hot water and bake at 350 degrees for 30 minutes, or until knife inserted in center comes out dry. Serve hot with Hollandaise Sauce. (Serves 6)

Pierre du Pont
Governor, Delaware

Edna Brock's B.B.Q. Beef Brisket

3 lbs. beef brisket
Place one sliced lemon and one medium onion sliced on the brisket. Wrap in heavy foil. Place in a shallow pan. The brisket should fit the pan loosely. Cook in oven six hours at 200 degrees. Cool and slice brisket thinly. Put B.B.Q. sauce on and put in oven two hours more, still wrapped in foil.

B.B.Q. SAUCE

2 c. catsup
2 Tbs. Worcesteshire sauce
2 tsp. prepared mustard
2 Tbs. Liquid smoke
4 Tbs. brown sugar
1/2 tsp. salt
2 garlic buds crushed (optional)
2 c. water

Donna Raymond
Docent, Will Rogers State Park

"The Stock Market has spoiled more appetites than bad cooking."

Chicken Cacciatora

1/4 cup olive oil
1 teaspoon salt
1 chicken (2-1/2 to 3 lbs., cut up)
2 onions, sliced
1/4 teaspoon pepper
2 cloves garlic, minced
1 can (1 lb.) Italian tomatoes
1 8 oz. can tomato sauce
1/2 teaspoon celery seed
1 teaspoon crushed, dried oregano
2 bay leaves
1/2 cup dry white wine

Heat oil in large deep skillet. Brown chicken in it. Remove chicken and keep hot. Cook onions and garlic in oil in skillet until tender. Add other ingredients, except wine, and blend. Cook 5 minutes. Return chicken to skillet. Cover and simmer 45 minutes. Add wine, and cook uncovered about 15 minutes or until chicken is tender. Arrange on hot platter. Skim any excess fat from sauce and remove bay leaves. Pour sauce over chicken and serve with spaghetti or noodles.

Serves 4 to 6.

Governor Thomas Judge

State of Montana

Rouladen

1 Slice Round Steak—1/4" thick (ask butcher to pound it)
Bacon
Onion
Salt
Mustard
Flour
Pepper

Trim out the bone and trim off all fat. Fry fat in skillet or electric skillet. Cut meat along veins, a few will be large, cut these in half.

Spread each piece with mustard, then a strip of bacon and some chopped onion. Roll into bundles and secure with 2 round toothpicks.

Dredge in flour and brown in fat already prepared. Usually it will be necessary to add some shortening.

A good brown crust adds to the flavor of this dish, so do not hurry this process. When all are browned, add water and cover pan. Simmer or bake for 1-1/2 or 2 hours, adding water as necessary.

I am sending you the recipe for Rouladen, and I hope you find it as delectable as I do. Best wishes and good luck on your cookbook to be used in the celebration of the birthday anniversary of Will Rogers.

Kindest personal regards,

Otis R. Bowen, M.D.
Governor
State of Indiana

Veal Parmigiana a la New Mexico

1 lb. thinly sliced veal cutlets (about 6)
1 egg, slightly beaten
3/4 cup fine dry seasoned bread crumbs
1/4 cup butter or margarine
1 16 oz. jar meatless spaghetti sauce
8 oz. mozzarella cheese, sliced
1 4 oz. can chopped green chili (more if desired)
1 4 oz. can mushrooms, drained
Grated Parmesan cheese

Preheat oven to 350 degrees.

Dip veal cutlets first in egg and then coat well with bread crumbs. Heat butter in skillet over moderately low heat; add veal and increase temperature to moderately high and brown veal well on both sides. Pour a layer of spaghetti sauce into bottom of a shallow 2-qt. baking dish. Arrange veal in a single layer over sauce. Spread green chili evenly over veal; then arrange sliced mozzarella over chili. Add drained mushrooms to remaining sauce and pour over cheese.

Sprinkle generously with Parmesan cheese and bake 35 minutes.

Serve with additional grated Parmesan cheese if desired. Serves 4.

I am enclosing a recipe for Veal Parmigiana a la New Mexico, which is a favorite of the Apodaca family. I hope your readers will enjoy it.

My best wishes for the success of this very worthwhile project.

Sincerely,

Jerry Apodaca
Governor

Chili and Beans

Grind 1 pound of round steak and one onion, salt to taste and saute until brown. Then add one can of tomatoes, one small can of pimiento (or take two fresh pimientos and skin, putting in hot oven or over gas jet until skins will come off easily) and chop fine. Cook this one hour. Then add two cans of red kidney beans, or soak two cups of red kidney beans overnight and cook over very slow fire.

Will Rogers

This receipe was first published in the Beverly Hills Woman's club cookbook in 1931. We thank the club for permission to reprint it.

Baked Ham

Use Swift's Premium. Score fat. Rub in all the brown sugar you can and stud with cloves. Make a paste of 8 cups of flour and water. Roll out and wrap ham. Save a piece of the dough to patch with as the steam will force holes through the dough. Put ham in roaster and add a little boiling water to keep from burning. Roast 5 or 6 hours, more if necessary depending on the size of ham. Break off dough; put ham in oven to brown. A little sweet pickle juice is good poured over ham before putting in oven to brown.

Will Rogers

Printed in the Beverly Hills Women's Cookbook — 1931

"When you get a group of women behind anything it is always a success."

Egg Timbales with Cheese Sauce

3 eggs
6 tablespoons whole milk
salt and pepper to taste

Beat eggs slightly, add milk, seasonings, and beat again. Butter timbale molds or custard cups, and fill two-thirds full. Place in pan of hot water and bake in 325 degree oven until firm—about 25 minutes.

SAUCE
1 tablespoon flour
1 tablespoon butter
2/3 cup milk (or beer)
3/4 lb. New York State sharp cheddar cheese, grated.

Melt butter, stir in flour until smooth, gradually add milk (or beer), add grated cheese and stir until smooth.

Turn out molds on serving platter and pour sauce over. Garnish with sauteed bacon and chopped parsley. Serve very hot.

Governor Hugh Carey
State of New York

A-1 Meatloaf

2 lbs. ground beef
2 tablespoons A-1 Steak Sauce
2 teaspoons salt
1 cup dry bread crumbs
2 eggs
3/4 cup milk
3 tablespoons parsley flakes
1 small onion, minced
1/4 cup shredded carrot

SAUCE
Mix 2 tablespoons A-1 Steak Sauce
1 can (8 oz.) tomato sauce

Mix all meatloaf ingredients together with one-half sauce mixture. Blend well. Pat meatloaf into 9 x 5 x 3" loaf pan, or shape into loaf in shallow baking pan. Spread remaining sauce mixture over top of meatloaf. Bake in 400 degree oven for one hour.

Mr. and Mrs. Willard Cruse
Will Rogers Park

Ham Loaf

1 lb. cured ham, chopped
1/2 lb. fresh ham, chopped
1-1/2 c. dry bread crumbs
2 eggs
3/4 c. milk
Pepper

Dressing:
1/2 c. water
1/4 c. sugar
1/4 c. vinegar
1 Tbs. mustard

Mix first group of ingredients well, form into loaf shape. Pour dressing over loaf, bake 1-1/2 hours at 350 degrees. Baste frequently. Serves 6.

Lt. Col. John H. Glenn, Jr.
U.S.M.C.
America's first orbital astronaut
February 20, 1962
John Glenn is also a U.S. Senator
from Ohio

"I like to make little jokes and kid about the Senators. They are a never-ending source of amusement, amazement and discouragement. But the rascals, when you meet 'em they are mighty nice fellows. It must be something in the office that makes 'em so honery sometimes. When you see what they do officially, you want to shoot 'em, but when one looks at you and grins so innocently, you kinder want to kiss him."

Wild Onions and Eggs

2 c. onions
6 Tbsp. bacon grease
1 c. water
6 beaten eggs

Clean and wash enough onions to make two cups, cut in one inch lengths. Put in a skillet with water, cook until tender. Pour off excess water. Season with bacon grease; cook five minutes. Add beaten eggs, stir until eggs are cooked. Add salt and pepper to taste. Serves 4.

Gazella Lane

Member of the Pocahontas Woman's Club of Claremore, Oklahoma

"We will never have true civilization until we have learned to recognize the rights of others."

"Chili Pie"

7 oz. can green roasted chilis
1 dozen eggs—well beaten
3/4 lb. grated cheese (sharp yellow cheese)
2 cans cream corn (optional)

Line baking dish, 3 to 4 qt. capacity, with green chilis, add cheese and well beaten eggs. Bake at 375 degrees 30-40 minutes.

If you want a more souffle type dish you can separate 1/2 the eggs—beat separately and fold in.

Patricia Z. Stephenson

Mrs. Stephenson is the daughter of Flo Ziegfeld and Billie Burke. The Ziegfelds were friends of the Rogers family, and of course Will Rogers worked in the "Ziegfeld Follies".

During World War I, Will Rogers was delivering his monologue in the Ziegfeld Follies one evening when a hatchet-faced woman in the ninth row called out, "Why aren't you in the Army?" Rogers gave everybody in the audience time to turn around and look at his heckler, then drawled, "For the same reason, madam, that you aren't in the Follies: physical disabilities."

Sarma

1 cup rice
1-1/2 pound ground pork
1 pound ground ham
1/2 pound ground beef
1 large onion
1/8 tsp. minced garlic
1 egg
1 large head soured cabbage
2 quarts sauerkraut
salt and pepper
strips of bacon

Place cabbage in large pan of water, core head and separate leaves. Wash each leaf and drain in colander. Wash sauerkraut and drain. Dice onion and brown lightly in fat, mix with meat, garlic, rice, seasonings and egg. Roll a generous portion of meat mixture in each leaf. When leaves are gone, shape rest of meat into balls. Cover bottom of large roaster pan with kraut and place rolls on top. If it is necessary to have more than one layer of rolls, place a layer of kraut between. End with a layer of kraut on top and place strips of bacon over kraut. Nearly cover with cold water. Bake covered at 350 degrees for about two hours. Approximately 22 Sarmas from 3 pounds of meat.

You will find enclosed a recipe for sarma, which represents Governor and Mrs. Perpich's ethnic background. The sarma is a Croatian main dish. It is a favorite of the Governor and his family.

Governor and Mrs. Rudy Perpich
of Minnesota

Stuffed Mushrooms Italiano

1 pound fresh mushrooms
1 stalk celery, chopped
1 small onion, minced
1 small clove garlic, crushed
1/4 cup Italian style bread crumbs
1/4 cup parmesan cheese
1 small egg, beaten
white wine, optional
salt and pepper

Wash mushrooms, break off stems and chop.

Arrange whole mushroom caps on baking sheet (for added flavor, sprinkle caps with white wine).

Bake in preheated oven (350 degrees) about 5 minutes while preparing filling.

Saute chopped stems, celery, onion and garlic in butter until onion is transparent, about 5 minutes.

Allow mushroom caps and saute to cool slightly.

Add breadcrumbs, cheese, egg and salt and pepper to saute.

Stuff mushroom caps and return to 350 degree oven for 10 minutes. Serve hot.

I am pleased to enclose a recipe for Stuffed Mushrooms Italiano which is a family favorite.

With best wishes,   Cordially,

Ella Grasso

Ella Grasso
Governor
State of Connecticut

Chicken Almond

Boil four chicken breasts, in ample water until tender. Add 2 bay leaves, 1 large onion, and 1 cup celery tops. Cook all at once. Retain broth. Cool chicken and cut in bite-size pieces.

Fry 2 lbs. sausage. Pour off fat. In small amount of the fat, fry one large bunch celery (about one cup), one bell pepper, two large onions, cut fine. Simmer until nearly tender.

In a large casserole pour 9 cups liquid (water and broth from cooking chicken), 2 cups rice (brown or white), one cup wild rice. 3 pkg. Lipton chicken noodle soup, 1 cup blanched almonds, 2 cans sliced mushrooms. Add all other ingredients. Cook covered, in 375 degree oven, 1-1/2 hours. Take cover off the last 10 minutes. Cover with slivered almonds. Stir twice while cooking.

Donna Raymond
Docent, Will Rogers State Park

Teriyaki Steak

Put in a blender:
1 T olive oil
1 onion
1 clove garlic
1/2 c brown sugar
1 c soy
1 t ginger or 1 T fresh sliced ginger
1/2 c water
Blend ingredients together.
Pour marinade over sirloin steak.

Broil 5 or 10 minutes, basting with marinade.

Harriet Axelrad
Docent, Will Rogers State Park

Quail

2 or 3 quail, cleaned and split down back
3 Tbsp. butter
2/3 cup sherry
1/3 cup worcestershire sauce
1/2 cup sour cream

Rinse quail well with salted water; brown in butter in frying pan. Combine sherry and sauce, pour over quail. Cover. Cook over low heat until tender, about 30 minutes, turning two or three times. Serve on toast. Blend sour cream with pan drippings until smooth; spoon over quail.

Serves 2 or 3.

This method can be used with Dove when Quail are not available.

Alice Karl
Docent, Will Rogers State Park

"The crime of taxation is not in the taking of it, it's in the way it's spent."

Quick Swedish Meatballs

Ground chopped beef in quantities to suit size of your group.

Add bread crumbs and seasoning to taste.

Roll very lightly into tiny meatballs and saute, preferably in their own fat, at least to start.

At the same time, open a can of cranberry sauce (either jellied or whole) and a can or jar of ready made spaghetti sauce (your favorite brand).

Blend together well, add meatballs, simmer, and serve on a bed of instant rice.

Milton J. Sharp
State of Pennsylvania

"If we can just improve their (women's) marksmanship, we can improve civilization. About every fourth fellow you meet nowadays ought to be shot."

"California Chili"

3 lbs. Round Steak (cut 1/2 inch cubes-trim fat)
2 onions—chopped
12 cloves garlic (finely chopped)
6 Tbs. olive oil
1 6 oz. can tomato paste
4 Tbs. Chili Powder
1 Tbs. Cumin
1-1/2 Tbs. paprika—1 Tbs. oregano—2 Tbs. salt—1 Tbs. red pepper
flakes
1/2 bell pepper
2 bay leaves
4 grindings black pepper corns
4 cup beef broth
5 cans small red beans

Heat 4 Tbsp. olive oil, in a large iron pot, add meat. Stir constantly
till lightly browned. Remove meat to a large casserole. Add remainder oil to iron pot. Cook onion and garlic in oil about 4 min. Remove
pot from heat. Add all other ingredients. Remove bay leaves after 20
minutes. Let simmer at least two hours.

Serve with a green salad and garlic-cheese bread.

Hal Roach

"You can always judge a town by the quality of the chili."

(B and O) Railroad Stew

1-1/2 lbs. stewing beef—sear (brown)
salt and pepper
1 large onion-diced-sear
Add one large can of solid packed tomatoes
Stew on low heat—add a bit of flour and water to thicken like gravy.
Last 10 minutes, add one package of frozen peas
Serve in a bed of mashed potatoes
Serves 4-5

If Will Rogers ever rode the train in his vaudeville days, he may have eaten this railroad stew. More than 50 years ago, my great uncle served this stew on the B and O Railroad. I believe it would not spill out of the dish if the train came to an emergency halt.

My grandmother doubled this recipe to serve her ten children.

Ethel Haydon
Past-President—Will Rogers Docents

"We can't go through life just eating cake all the time."

Mrs. Rogers' Southern Green Beans

2 lbs. string beans
1/2 lb. salt pork
1 medium onion, peeled
1 quart water
Salt and pepper

Cut beans approximately 1-1/2 inches in length. Cube and brown salt pork. Bring water to boil, add beans, salt pork, onion and salt and pepper to taste. Simmer slowly 2 to 3 hours.

Submitted by Mr. Emil Sandmeier who worked for the Rogers family for many years and reports that very simple dishes were served at the Ranch House.

"Of course, the Mother I know the most about is the Mother of our little group. She has been for 22 years trying to raise to maturity, four children, three by birth and one by marriage. While she hasent done a good job, the poor soul has done all that mortal human could do with the material she has had to work with."

Will Rogers "Good Old Oklahoma Beans"

2 lbs. small white navy beans
1 generous ham hock
1 medium onion, peeled
Salt and pepper

Soak beans over night in cold water. In the morning, drain and cover with fresh water. Bring to boil, add ham hock, onion, salt and pepper to taste. Simmer slowly for 4 hours. Add more water, if necessary so beans will be kind of soupy. Each serving should include a partion of ham.

Emil Sandmeier

Will Rogers Ranch

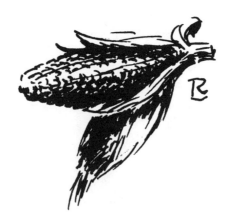

"Left New York at ! P.M. today; am at Cleveland at 5 P.M., and will be in Beverly tomorrow night for corn bread and beans."

Lasagne

1 lb. ground beef
1 clove garlic, minced
2 tblsp salad oil
1 can (1 lb. 4 oz.) solid pack tomatoes
1 can (8 oz.) tomato sauce
1 tsp. salt
1/2 tsp pepper
1/2 tsp. oregano
1/2 lb. lasagne noodles, cooked just tender
1 lb. ricotta or dry cottage cheese
1/2 cup grated Parmesan cheese
1/2 lb. Mozzarella cheese, sliced

Brown beef and garlic in oil, stirring with a fork. Add tomatoes, first draining off half the juice; add tomato sauce and seasonings. Simmer for 30 min. Cook noodles, drain and rinse. Cover bottom of a large greased baking dish with 1-1/2 cups of beef mixture. Cover the beef mixture with a single layer of noodles. Spread 1/2 of the ricotta cheese on the noodles, sprinkle with 1/2 the Parmesan cheese and place over this 1/3 of the Mozzarella cheese. Repeat. Top with remaining beef mixture and mozzarella. Bake in 350 oven for 45 min. Let stand 15 min. after removing from oven. Cut into squares.

Willard Cruse
Will Rogers Park groundskeeper and
horticulturist since 1953

"Wherever you find poor soil, you will always find politics."

Baked Chicken Breasts

(Prepare ahead and bake tomorrow)

Deboned Chicken Breasts
Cheese (Longhorn)
Sour Cream
Bacon
Toothpicks
Salt, Pepper (Garlic powder optional)
Figure at least 2 pieces of chicken per person.

The night before prepare the following:
Pull outer skin off chicken. Lay chicken out flat and season both sides. Lay chicken with the inside toward you. Cut cheese hunks approximately 2 in. long and 1/2 inch wide and tall. Place in middle of the chicken. Cut bacon strips in half and get toothpicks handy. Starting with the smallest end of the chicken, roll toward the middle (with cheese inside) and past the other end. Wrap the bacon strip around the middle and pin with toothpicks. Place on a cooky sheet approximately 2 inches apart. Heap 2 generous tablespoons of sour cream on top in the middle of each and refrigerate until the following day. Must set at least 8 hours.

The following day preheat oven to 350 degrees and bake for 1 hour. Chicken will have a pink color like shrimp.

Don Towne
Docent—Will Rogers State Park

"This is an age of progress. Live fast and die quick. The human side of anything cant compare with so-called progress."

Baked Stuffed Shrimp

Buy frozen jumbo shrimp (allow 4 to a serving). Thaw them; drain them. Flatten shrimp in a buttered shallow baking pan. Top with following dressing:

1 cup rolled cracker crumbs
1 cup finely crushed potato chips
1 stick butter or margarine melted
1 pint scallops, put through food grinder, raw

Season with garlic salt, onion salt, just a dash celery salt.

Enough milk to make light and fluffy dressing.

Put generous amount of dressing on each flattened-out shrimp. This is enough for 16 to 20 jumbo shrimp. Sprinkle generously with grated Parmesan cheese. Bake at 350 degrees about 20 minutes or until shrimp meat has turned white.

James B. Longley

Governor

State of Maine

Beef Teriyaki

2 lbs. sirloin tip or 4-5 steaks
2/3 C soy sauce
1/2 C sugar
1 t monosodium glutamate
2 T green onions, chopped
1 t fresh ginger root, grated
5 cloves garlic, chopped
1 T sesame oil (optional)
1 T sesame seeds, crushed (optional)

Combine all ingredients except beef. Additional sugar may be added to sweeten.

Marinate beef a half hour before grilling.

Governor George R. Ariyoshi
State of Hawaii

"Hawaii is the only place I know where they lay flowers on you while you are alive."

Layered Tortilla Pie

1 pound ground beef
1 medium onion, chopped
1 clove garlic, minced
1 tablespoon butter or margarine
1 (8-ounce) can tomato sauce
1 (2-1/4 ounce) can sliced ripe olives, drained
1 tablespoon chili powder
1 teaspoon salt
1/4 teaspoon pepper
6 corn tortillas, buttered
2 cups shredded longhorn Cheddar cheese
1/2 cup water

Brown beef, onion and garlic in butter. Drain. Add tomato sauce, olives, chili powder, salt and pepper. In a round 2-quart casserole, alternate layers of tortillas, meat sauce and 1-1/2 cups cheese. Sprinkle remaining 1/2 cup cheese over top. Pour water at edge of casserole into bottom. Cover and bake at 400 degrees 25 minutes. Uncover and let stand 5 minutes before cutting in wedges. Makes 4 servings.

Ruth Bloch
Docent—Will Rogers State Park

"Happiness and contentment is progress. In fact that's all progress is."

Stuffed Ham Seville

1 can mandarin oranges
1/4 Cup orange marmalade
1/4 teaspoon ground ginger
3 Cups cooked rice
1/4 Cup chopped pecans (optional)
3 tablespoons sliced onion
1/4 Cup mayonnaise or salad dressing
6 large thin slices of baked ham.

(1) Drain liquid from mandarin oranges. Cook liquid rapidly until reduced by half; then stir in marmalade and ginger.

(2) Set aside 12 mandarin orange segments. Mix with remaining other ingredients (except ham) in a bowl. Spoon about 3/4 Cup onto each slice of ham. Fold ham over to cover filling and place in a shallow baking dish. Brush with part of hot orange sauce.

(3) Bake in a moderate 350 degree oven, brushing with remaining orange sauce for about 25 minutes. Garnish with saved mandarin orange segments. Bake 5 minutes longer.

> Governor David L. Boren
> State of Oklahoma

Will was born in Oklahoma on November 4, 1879.

"Politicians can do more funny things naturally than I can think of to do purposely."

Lobster Ragout

1 lb. lobster meat (canned chunk)
1 can condensed cream of chicken soup
3/4 cup light cream
1 can chicken gumbo soup—condensed
1/2 tsp. Worcestershire sauce
1 tsp. curry powder
1/2 cup dry sherry wine

1. Put lobster meat, both soups, light cream, worcestershire sauce, curry powder and sherry into top of double boiler on chafing dish over water. Mix thoroughly . . . but gently . . . so as not to break lobster chunks.

2. Cook gently until the curry is cooked and hot. (It is best to blend curry powder with a little butter or warm water for easier blending.)

3. Serve on hot plates over toast points.
Serves four (4).

If you do not use toast points . . . do serve crisp French bread. A green salad goes well. Crab meat may be substituted for lobster.

I have enclosed Mrs. Byrne's recipe for LOBSTER RAGOUT which has been a favorite of the family for many years.

Sincerely,

Brendan T. Byrne
Governor
State of New Jersey

Chicken Enchiladas Babbitt

4 Chicken Breasts (or 1 whole chicken) cooked, deboned & cubed
12 Corn Tortillas
1 8 oz. can chopped Green Chilis
1 can Cream of Chicken soup
1 can Cream of Mushroom soup
(add 1/2 t. ground Coriander to soups and heat)
1 large onion, diced
1/2 lb. Cheddar cheese, grated
1/2 lb. Monterey Jack cheese, grated

Line 2-3 qt. casserole with Tortillas after dipping in warm oil. Layer cubed chicken, green chili, diced onion, undiluted soups mixtures, then cheese. Repeat layering until ingredients are used, topping off with cheese. Bake in 350 degree approximately 1 hour.

(Individual enchilladas may be made by filling one corn tortilla with the ingredients, lay side-by-side in shallow baking pan, cover with soup mix and grated cheese and bake 20-30 mins.) Top with chopped green onions before serving if you like things spicy!

Raul Castro
Governor—State of Arizona

"The best way to judge just how good a man is, is to find out how he stands around his home and among his kind of people."

Julian's Chili

2 lbs. ground beef
1 medium onion
1 pkg. spaghetti
2 cans chili beans
3/4 cup sugar
2 cans tomato paste
1 qt. home-canned tomato juice
4 to 6 tsp. chili powder
1/2 cup red wine
Salt and garlic to taste

Brown ground beef and onions together. Cook spaghetti in three quarts salt water: Retain water for part of liquid. Add other ingredients. Simmer for 1-1/2 hours. Add red wine 30 minutes before done.

Note: Except for the addition of the wine, which is Charlann's suggestion, this is the recipe Governor Carroll used when he cooked for his brothers and sisters as a boy.

A favorite recipe of

Governor & Mrs. Julian M. Carroll of Kentucky

Governor Ray's All-time Favorite—
Bouillabaisse

3 cans (1 pound 4 ounces each) stewed tomatoes
2 large onions, chopped
4 cups celery, chopped into 1-inch strips
1 green pepper, chopped
Juice of 2 oranges and 1 Tbsp grated orange rind
1 small can (about 3 oz.) chicken soup base
Salt and pepper to taste
Assorted seasonings (1/2 tsp. each garlic, tarragon, dill weed or dill seed) tied into cheesecloth bag
1 Tbsp parsley
1 cup of your favorite red wine (dry)
2 to 4 pounds fresh salmon, cut into chunks
2 to 4 pounds fresh halibut or other white fish, cut into chunks
1 to 2 pounds each raw scallops, frozen shrimp, whole well-scrubbed clams and any other raw seafood
Legs, claws and body chunks of fresh crab

Into large heavy soup kettle mix tomatoes, onions, celery, green pepper, juice and rind of oranges, salt, pepper, parsley and assorted seasonings in cheesecloth bag. Cover kettle and bring to a slow boil. Continue to simmer for one hour. Add red wine.

20 minutes before serving add all the fish and seafood EXCEPT CRAB.
5 minutes before serving add the crab.

Be sure Bouillabaisse is kept at full simmer until serving. Serve in large soup bowls accompanied by hot garlic french bread.

Large napkins or small tea towels are a necessity. Be prepared for 2 to 3 servings per person.

Recipe serves 8 to 12.

This is a fun recipe . . . Keep tasting and testing . . . Add your own favorite

seasonings. Important . . . ! . . . do not simmer away too much of the soup
. . . it may be very necessary to add more liquid . . . use water or tomato
juice.

I am happy to enclose my favorite bouillabaisse recipe for the Will Roger's
cookbook. I am grateful for your invitation to visit his California ranch
house.

Sincerely,

Dixy Lee Ray
Governor
State of Washington

Hungarian Goulash with Noodles

Serves 25
5 Lbs. Beef Rump or Round, cubed
1 Qt. Onion, finely chopped
1 Clove Garlic, finely chopped

Brown the meat, onion and garlic in suet or vegetable oil.

Add:
1-1/2 Teaspoon dry mustard
1/4 Cup Paprika
1/2 Cup and 1 Tablespoon Brown Sugar
1 Tablespoon salt
1 Cup Worcestershire Sauce
1 Tablespoon Vinegar
2 Cups Catsup
1 Qt. Water
1 Qt. Beef Consomme

Mix, cook, add to meat and simmer until tender.

Strain meat and thicken juice with 2 cups plus 1 tablespoon flour, mixed with cold water. Return meat to gravy.

Cook *wide* noodles until slightly underdone. Then divide into baking pans and mix with the meat mixture.

Reheat pans about 1/2 hour before serving to guests. If they stand long, mix with a bit of water and reheat.

This is one of our family favorites and is highly representative of the State of North Dakota since we are a leading producer of beef.

I would be happy to have the opportunity sometime to visit Will Rogers ranch home. I'm sure that would be a very intersting tour.

Sincerely,

Arthur A. Link
Governor
North Dakota

Rice Dressing

2 pounds lean ground beef
1 cup chopped white onions
1 cup chopped celery
1 cup chopped sweet green peppers
Dry mustard, salt, pepper and cayenne pepper to taste
1 cup short-grain rice

Saute ground meat in large, heavy saucepan (black cast iron, preferably) until browned well. Add half of the chopped ingredients and seasonings. Continue to cook over low fire for about one hour, keeping moist by adding small amounts of water as needed.

In the meantime, cook rice—1 cup of rice/two cups of water.

After meat mixture has simmered one hour, add remaining chopped ingredients and continue to cook approximately 45 minutes, adding again, small amounts of water as needed.

When ready to serve, combine rice with meat mixture and serve at once.

Thank you very much for advising me of the cookbook the Docent Organization is preparing in commemoration of Will Roger's 100th Birthday. I am pleased to enclose my favorite recipe to be used in this cookbook and I am honored by your request.

Best wishes.

Cordially,

Edwin Edwards
State of Louisiana

Master's Pork Chops

6 1" thick pork chops
1/2 teaspoon accent
1 teaspoon salt
1-1/2 cups finely crushed butterly crackers (round)
2 onions finely chopped
1/4 cup flour
1/4 teaspoon pepper
1 egg slightly beaten
2 tablespoon water
1 teaspoon butter
1 clove garlic minced

1. Prepare sauce. 2. Coat chops with a mixture of flour (seasoned with salt and pepper), dip both sides in a blend of egg, water, finally coating with cracker crumbs. 3. Brown chops on both sides in hot butter in a large skillet. Remove browned chops and keep warm. 4. Add onions, garlic to fat remaining in skillet cooking until onions are soft. 5. Return chops to skillet. Pour sauce over all, cover and cook over low heat about 50 minutes or until meat is tender, baste occasionally during cooking. 6. Remove chops to a warm platter. Pour sauce into gravy boat; pass at table.

SAUCE
1/2 cup lightly packed brown sugar
1 cup water
1 cup catsup
3 slices lemon
1 tablespoon bottled brown bouquet sauce
2 teaspoons dry mustard
2 tablespoons cider vinegar
3 oz. (1 pkg.) cream cheese
1 tablespoon butter

Mix brown sugar, dry mustard in a saucepan, stir in the water, vinegar and a blend of catsup, cream cheese. Add lemon slices, butter. Heat thoroughly, stirring occasionally. When ready to use, remove from heat and mix in the bottled bouquet sauce.

I usually mix everything in the blender except the lemon slices and butter. It's creamier.

Jim and Kathy Peat

Maintenance Supervisor,

Will Rogers State Park

"There is nothing like congenial friends to just sit around with nothing in particular to knock and a good word for all."

73

Grilled Leg of Lamb with Avǵolemonó

large leg of lamb, boned
2/3 c olive oil
4 T lemon juice
1 t salt
1/2 t pepper
2 T parsley, chopped
1-1/2 t oregano
3 bay leaves, crumbled
1 medium onion, thinly sliced
3 cloves garlic, thinly sliced

When you ask your butcher to bone the leg of lamb for you, ask him to trim the fell (the parchment—like covering) and fat as well. When you get home, remove all the little bits of fat and fell which the butcher missed. Set aside while you prepare the marinade.

In a glass, enamel, or stainless steel container large enough to hold the lamb place the olive oil, lemon juice, salt, pepper, parsley, oregano, and bay leaves. Whisk together until well combined, then add the onion and garlic. Stir around just enough to distribute the onion and garlic evenly. Place the lamb on top of the marinade, then turn it over once or twice to make sure it's well coated. Spoon a little of the marinade on top of the lamb and cover with plastic wrap. Let marinate at room temperature, preferably for 24 hours (minimum should be 12 hours). Turn over half way through marinating period. You may refrigerate it from time to time if the temperature of your kitchen is warmer than usual—just be sure that the lamb is at room temperature just before you grill it.

Allow 30 minutes for grilling the lamb—I say "grilling". I prefer the extra flavor which a charcoal fire gives to the lamb. The charcoal should be started about 30-40 minutes before the lamb is placed on the grill or until the charcoal is coated with gray ash. Grill for 15 minutes on one side, brushing with the marinade 2 or 3 times to prevent drying, then turn and grill for another 15 minutes, again brushing with the marinade a few times. Remove to carving board and carve in slices against the grain of the meat. Arrange the slices in an overlapping fashion in a serving dish, then pour over the juice accumulated when carving and any remaining marinade (strained). Serve immediately. Pass the avgolemono sauce separately in a heated sauce dish. Serves 6-8.

AVGOLEMONÓ SAUCE

(Optional)
3 eggs
juice of 2 lemons
2 t arrowroot (may need more)
1/2 t salt
generous dash of cayenne pepper
1 c hot chicken stock
1 T. parsley, finely chopped
5-6 mint leaves, finely chopped

Beat the eggs until just combined. Whisk in the lemon juice, arrowroot, salt, and pepper. Very slowly at first, add the hot chicken stock, whisking constantly. Over a moderately low heat, continue whisking the sauce until thickened. Keep warm by placing over—not in—hot water. Just before serving, stir in the parsley and mint.

Tom McKiernan—
1971 Citizen of the Year
Pacific Palisades

Wild Rice Hot Dish

1 cup wild rice
3 medium chopped onions
1 diced green pepper
1 pound ground beef

Brown onions, pepper and beef in 2 tablespoons butter. Do not season.
1 can cream of mushroom soup
1 can mushrooms and juice
3 to 4 ounces soy sauce
1 small can sliced water chestnuts
3 cups water

Add soup, mushrooms, soy sauce, chestnuts and water to ground beef mixture and mix thoroughly.

Drain wild rice and mix with other ingredients. Place in casserole. 1/8 cup cashews may be sprinkled on top if desired. Bake 1-1/2 hours at 350 degrees. Makes 6 average servings.

Walter F. Mondale

Walter Mondale
Vice President of
the United States

Roast Pheasant

1 or 2 pheasant
1 stick butter
1/2 onion, chopped
flour, salt and pepper
1/2 cup crisco
1 can mushroom soup

Cut up bird(s) - cut breast off bone and separate into four (4) steaks. If birds are in good supply it is nicer to use just the breast and legs. Dredge pieces in seasoned flour; brown in mixture of butter and crisco. Place browned pieces in roasting pan. Cook onions in same pan until limp and golden, adding more butter or crisco if needed. Add mushroom soup to onions, mix well and pour over pheasant in roaster. Rinse onion pan with a little water and add. Cover roaster, cook in 325 degree oven about 2 hours—watch the last half hour so the birds don't dry too much.

Optional:
Add 1 clove garlic minced, 1/4 tsp. rosemary, 1/4 tsp parsley, 1/4 cup white wine and 1/2 cup water to pan with onions and cook 5 minutes, then add mushroom soup and finish recipe. Omit rinsing the pan with water if this method is used.

Alice Karl
Docent—Will Rogers State Park

"It will take America fifteen years steady taking care of our own business and letting everybody else's alone to get us back to where everybody speaks to us again."

Joe's Fried Chicken

1 Chicken (clean and cut into pieces)
Mix:
2 to 3 cups milk
2 unbeaten eggs
Soak cleaned chicken in milk and egg mixture for one-half hour.

Remove chicken, season with salt and pepper, sprinkle with paprika, roll in mixture of two parts crushed corn flakes and one part flour. Deep fry in pure vegetable oil.

If you wish, you may mix the salt, pepper, paprika, crushed corn flakes and flour together, and roll chicken in mixture.

Governor Joseph P. Teasdale
State of Missouri

"That's what makes us a great country. The little things are serious and the big ones are not."

Lorie's Enchiladas

Sauce: Heat together.
2 1 lb. 12 oz. cans tomato puree
1/2 t salt
onion flakes
pepper and garlic to taste
1/4 t oregano
1 t sugar
(Enchilada sauce may be used for one or both cans of tomato puree)

1 pkg. cheddar cheese, grated
1/2-1 pkg. Monterey Jack Cheese, grated
12 corn tortillas, fried for a few seconds one at a time in hot oil until soft.
Dip in sauce and fill with cheese mixture and a few ripe olives, sliced.
Place side by side rolled up and seam side down in a 13x9x2 pan.

Pour remaining sauce over top. Sprinkle with cheese and olives.

Heat 15-20 minutes in 350 degree oven. Serves 6.

Ground beef, chicken, or turkey may be used along with the cheese.

I sometime make extra sauce to pour over the top after the enchiladas have been cooked.

John Falk
Will Rogers Park Aide

Princeton denies that they were rough with Harvard in football. They say they were firm but never rough, that it wasn't necessary.

Seasoning for Venison Steaks, Fish, Chicken and Beef

2 tsp. onion salt
1/4 tsp. seasoned pepper
1 Tbsp. dried chives
1 Tbsp. chervil
2 tsp. seasoned salt
1 Tbsp. parsley
1 Tbsp. marjoram leaves
1 Tbsp. tarragon leaves
2 envelopes instant chicken broth or 1 jar instant chicken broth

Place all ingredients in blender, mix until there is a fine powder. Store in tightly covered jar. When ready to use mix 4 tsp. of seasoning with 1 cup of flour, dredge steaks in flour mixture. Brown steaks in hot shortening. This mixture may be used with fish, chicken and beef too.

Alice Karl
Docent—Will Rogers State Park

"There is still a lot of monkey in us. Throw anything you want in our cage and we will give it serious consideration."

Parsley and Parmesan Chicken

Marinate 6-7 chicken breasts (boned and halved) with 1/2 cup Italian Dressing for several hours.
1 egg and 2 Tbsp. water
1 cup grated Parmesan Cheese
2/3 cup Italian seasoned bread crumbs
4 tsp. snipped parsley
1 tsp. salt
1 tsp. paprika
1/2 tsp. pepper
Dip in egg and water mixture, then in dry mixture.
Place in baking sheet, lightly greased. Bake in 350 degree oven 40 minutes.

Edith Cooper
Docent—Will Rogers State Park

"Everybody is ignorant only on different subjects."

Pepper Shrimp

What You Need:
One pound to one pound and a half of shelled and deveined shrimp
2-1/2 tablespoons of soy sauce
1 tablespoon Chinese rice wine
8 scallions cut up
1-1/2 tablespoons peeled and finely chopped ginger root
1-1/2 teaspoons of fresh garlic cut up
1-1/2 teaspoons sugar
1 teaspoon salt
1-1/2 teaspoons crushed red pepper flakes
3 tablespoons ketchup
1 tablespoon of cornstarch dissolved in 2 tablespoons of cold chicken stock
3 tablespoons of peanut oil or any other cooking oil

What You Do:
Some places where you buy shrimp will clean and devein them for you . . . other places are not so kind! Whatever the case may be, upon completion of cleaning their little bodies, wash with cold water and then pat dry with a paper towel. Keep them in the refrigerator until you are ready to use them.

When you are cooking Japanese or Chinese food, it is wise to keep all items in easy reach and make sure everything is chopped prior to starting dish.

It is best to cook this dish in a wok, but if one is not available, you can use a skillet . . . just make sure it is a large one. Place it over a very high heat for about twenty seconds. Pour in your 3 tablespoons of oil and swirl it around the wok or skillet for about 15 seconds. Sometimes the oil starts smoking. If it does, reduce the heat. Now add the scallions, ginger, garlic and red pepper flakes and stir for approximately 15 seconds, and then put in the shrimp. Cook, while constantly stirring, for around three minutes or until the shrimp turn pink and are firm. I have found that it is almost impossible to overcook the shrimp . . . and let's face it, a cooked shrimp usually tastes better than a raw one . . . at least to me! Now add the Chinese rice wine, ketchup, soy sauce, salt and sugar . . . stir it all up good. Now, make sure the cornstarch and chicken stock are mixed well and add it to the dish. Keep stirring . . . The mixture will thicken and the shrimp will have a glazed coat. Once this happens, the dish is done and should be served immediately. I always serve it over rice . . . but pure shrimp lovers may not care for it in this fashion. If you prepare everything in the afternoon, it is a great dish for company because actual cooking time is very short.

Edith Cooper
Docent—Will Rogers State Park

"Diplomats are just as essential to starting a war as Soldiers are for finishing it."

Betsy's Texas Pot Roast

Serves 4-6 generously
1 5 lb. 7-bone roast
3 tbs. butter
1 c. flour
2 — 2-1/2 tbs. seasoned salt (Lowry's)
2 tbs. Accent
1/5th bottle of sweet vermouth
2 5 oz. bottles of horseradish (yes, 2 - don't worry, horseradish turns sweet and loses its pungency)
2 1 lb. cans of new potatoes - optional
1 lb. fresh carrots, or other vegetables - optional

Combine flour and seasonings - dredge roast thoroughly in flour mixture on all sides.

Melt butter in large Dutch oven till slightly brown - add roast and brown thoroughly on all sides - to a real rich dark brown - remove roast from pan and add remaining flour mixture to drippings - stir well and brown the flour mixture - replace roast in pan.

Add vermouth (less one glass for the cook!) and enough water to cover meat - simmer covered for two hours - add one bottle of horseradish - simmer another two hours adding water as needed to keep roast covered with liquid - add second bottle of horseradish.

Continue simmering till bones can be easily removed from meat - about another hour. Tastes better the longer it cooks! About one-half hour before serving add potatoes and vegetables as desired.

This is an old recipe from Barry's family as served in Athens, Texas; we thought it most appropriate for a Will Rogers memorial cookbook.

Barry & Anna Cool
Mrs. Cool— 1961 Citizen of the Year
Pacific Palisades

"Texas starts entertaining you when you hit the state line."

Tijuana Hamburger Torte

1 lb. ground beef
1 can stewed tomatoes
1 can chopped green chilies
12 corn tortillas
1 med. onion, chopped
1 can tomato sauce
1 package taco season mix
1 lb. cheddar cheese, grated

Brown beef, onions in skillet. Add stewed tomatoes, tomato sauce, green chilies, and taco mix. Combine thoroughly, simmer 10 to 15 min. Place about 1/4 cup mixture in the bottom of a 9 x 13 baking dish. Place 2 tortillas side by side on the meat mixture. Top each with meat mixture, then cheese. Repeat until each stack contains 6 tortillas layered with meat mixture and cheese. Bake 350 degrees for 20 to 25 min. or until cheese is bubbly. Cut each torte (stack) into quarters with sharp knife before serving. Yield 4 to 6 servings.

Jim and Kathy Peat
Maintenance Supervisor
Will Rogers State Park

"Always remember this, that as bad as we sometimes think our government is run, it's the best run I ever saw."

Chicken Quarré

4 pieces chicken breasts, boned and skinned
4 pieces chicken thighs, boned and skinned
4 pieces chicken legs, boned and skinned
Combine:
2 pkgs. Uncle Ben's Wild Rice
3/4 c sherry wine
1/2 t Italian herb seasoning
1/2 t parsley
2 cans cream of mushroom soup

Cover bottom of a flat roasting pan with above. Gently place pieces of chicken on top of rice mixture; sprinkle chicken with 1/2 pkg. of well-mixed, dried onion soup mix.

Cover tightly and bake in medium oven 350 degrees for 1-1/2 hours. Serves six.

Lisa Quarré
Will Rogers Park Aide

"I can always find the good in people, beyond that, I did not bother."

Barbecued Trout

To keep fish fresh in appearance and aroma brush inside and out with lemon juice before refrigerating.

Trout marinade:
1/4 c vegetable oil
1/2 c cooking sherry
1/2 c soy sauce
1 T lemon juice
1 clove of garlic, crushed
Blend well before using.

Place trout in a shallow pan and cover with marinade. Let stand at least one hour. Place trout on the grill and barbecue until done, 10-15 minutes.

Jack Thompson
Maintenance Worker 1
Will Rogers State Park

"No man can be condemned for owning a dog. As long as he has a dog he has a friend and the poorer he gets the better friend he has."

Roast Loin of Pork/Orange Sauce with Almond Stuffed Onions

1 pork center loin roast (about 5 pounds)
1/2 clove garlic
1 teaspoon dill weed
1 teaspoon salt

Heat oven to 325 degrees. Rub meat with garlic and dill weed; sprinkle with salt. Place meat fat side up in shallow roasting pan. Insert meat thermometer in center of thickest part of meat, away from fat or bone.
Roast uncovered 2-1/2 to 3 hours to internal temperature of 170 degrees. Allow to stand at room temperature 15 to 20 minutes before carving.

ORANGE SAUCE
1 can (6 oz.) orange juice concentrate
1/2 cup light corn syrup
2 tablespoons catsup

Combine all ingredients in a small sauce pan. Bring to a boil; simmer until slightly thickened. Serve as a sauce over roast pork or use as a glaze during last hour of roasting period.

ALMOND STUFFED ONIONS
6 medium onions, about 3 inches in diameter
3/4 cup coarsely chopped almonds
1-1/2 cups croutons
3/4 teaspoons salt
1/4 teaspoon pepper
1/4 teaspoon sage
1/8 teaspoon thyme
1/4 cup melted butter
1 cup apple juice

Cut a thin slice off root end of each onion; cut a 1/4-inch slice off opposite end. Carefully remove center of each onion with vegetable parer or melon ball cutter, leaving a 3/8-inch shell (at least 3 rings). Arrange onion shells in ungreased 2-quart casserole.

Toss almonds, croutons, salt, pepper, sage, thyme and butter. Fill each onion shell with stuffing. Spoon any remaining stuffing on top of onions. Pour apple juice around onions. Put casserole in oven about 40 minutes before roast pork is done. Bake covered 40 minutes. Uncover and bake until tender, about 20 minutes longer while roast is standing.

Governor Ed Herschler
Governor of Wyoming

Lamb Stew

3 lbs. boneless lamb (in cubes or one piece)
1/4 c flour
2 t salt
1/2 t pepper
1 t paprika
1/2 t garlic powder
3 Ts fat
1 c diced onions
1 c canned tomato sauce
1 c boiling water
1 bay leaf
1 c sliced green pepper
3 potatoes, peeled and sliced
1 package frozen mixed vegetables

Cut lamb into cubes if necessary. Mix together the flour and spices. Lightly roll the lamb in mixture. Brown in fat together with diced onions. Add the tomato sauce, water, bay leaf and green peppers. Cover and cook over low heat 1-1/2 hours. Add the potatoes and vegetables. Cook another twenty minutes. Remove bay leaf. Serves 6-8.

Mitzi Cummings Fielding

Eggplant Palmagiano

1 eggplant
8 oz. mozzarella chese
2 eggs
1/2 cup flour
1/4 tsp. salt
1 tsp. garlic salt
2 tsps. sweet basil
1/3 cup oil
1 pint spaghetti sauce
1 romano cheese

Remove skin of eggplant and slice to about 1/8 to 1/4 inch. Combine flour, salt, garlic salt and sweet basil. Dip each slice into milk, then in flour mixture and lastly in beaten eggs. Fry in oil on each side till golden brown. Spread a bit of sauce on bottom of round pizza pan or baking dish. Spread fried eggplant and top with sauce and sprinkle with romano cheese. Repeat with another layer of eggplant, and romano cheese. Top with sliced mozzarella cheese. Bake at 350 degrees for 15 or 20 minutes or until cheese is melted but not browned. SERVE HOT!

J. Joseph Garrahy
Governor of Rhode Island

Herb's Chili Recipe

3 lbs. diced lean beef
1/4 cup olive oil (enough to brown the meat)
6 cups water
6 tablespoons chili powder (3 oz.)
3 teaspoons salt
10 cloves finely chopped garlic
1 teaspoon ground cumin
1 teaspoon marjoram or oregano
1 teaspoon red pepper (cayenne)
1 tablespoon sugar
3 tablespoons paprika (1-1/2 oz.)
3 tablespoons flour
6 tablespoons corn meal
6 chili tepines (or to taste - 1 or 2 make a lot of difference)

Brown meat in hot olive oil in dutch oven or large pot. Add remaining ingredients, stir frequently while simmering over low heat (just enough heat to keep it bubbling). Add corn meal slowly while sitring constantly (so it thickens smoothly). Allow to simmer 2 to 3 hours (until meat is *very* tender). Add beans and simmer for at least another hour.

2 pounds Pinto beans. Cook separately according to recipe on package. When the beans are added to the chili add liquid from the beans as desired.

Herbert L. Heinze
Calif. State Park Manager IV

Szechwan Beef

1 lb. Beef Loin
2 T. Wine
2 T. Soy Sauce
6 T Oil
1 cup Shredded Celery
3 Chili Peppers
1 tsp. Pressed Garlic
1/2 t. Salt
1/2 t. Sugar

Shred beef and marinate in wine and soy sauce for 10 minutes. Heat 3 T. oil and saute celery over high heat until coated with oil. Remove to plate. Seed and shred chili peppers, heat 3 T. oil and saute beef, peppers and garlic over high heat. When the beef changes color, add salt, sugar and celery. Serve hot over rice or Chinese noodles.

Note: Ideally this is better cooked in a wok, but if none is available, any large, shallow frying pan with curved sides will do.

Nini Holmes Lyddy
Docent—Will Rogers State Park

"Well, all I know is what I read in the papers."

Sesame Seed Chicken Wings

3 lb.s chicken wings
1/4 c. flour
1/2 c. cornstarch
1/4 c. sugar
1-1/2 t. salt
1/2 t. MSG
5 t. soy sauce
2 eggs
2 green onions, thinly sliced
2 cloves garlic, crushed
1 T. sesame seeds

Cut wings at the joint and discard the last joint. Combine all other ingredients. Marinate a minimum of two hours. Heat oil to 350 degrees, and fry until golden brown.

Gail and David Sears
District Interpretive Specialist
California State Parks

Crab Imperial

1 lb. crabmeat (preferably backfin)
2 tbs. margarine or butter
2 tbs. flour
3/4 cup milk
1 egg, beaten
1 hard-cooked egg, chopped fine
1 tbs. mayonnaise
6 drops Worcestershire sauce
1/2 tsp. dry mustard
1/2 tsp. parsley flakes
1/4 tsp. seafood seasoning
1 tsp. salt
1/4 tsp. pepper
1/2 cup bread crumbs
1/4 cup melted margarine or butter
Pimiento for garnish

Remove cartilage from crabmeat, and put in large bowl. Melt margarine or butter over low heat. Add flour and stir to make paste. Add milk and cook slowly, stirring constantly, until thickened. Reserve 6 tablespoons white sauce; add remainder to crabmeat, along with raw egg, hard-cooked egg, mayonnaise, Worcestershire sauce, mustard, parsley flakes, seafood seasning, salt and pepper. Mix gently but thoroughly. Put crabmeat mixture into 6 baking shells or ramekins. Top each with breadcrumbs, then melted margarine or butter, then reserved white sauce. Add pimiento strips for garnish.

Bake at 350 degrees F., 15 to 20 minutes or until browned on top. Makes 6 servings.

Harry Hughes
Governor, Maryland

Fettucini Facile (Easy) "Ala Raymond Burr"

Salt water with 1 to 2 tsps. bring to a boil. Add one package imported Fettucini noodles. When water returns to a boil, cook for 10-12 minutes. Drain in colander.

While noodles are draining, melt 1/4 pound of butter in the noodle pot.

Add:
1-1/2 cartons of sour cream (24 oz.)
3 tsps. of Accent
3 tsps. freshly ground pepper
2 tsps. of salt
MIX WELL

Return drained noodles to pot—with 2 wooden spoons, fold into butter mixture.

Add 4 cups of imported grated Parmesan cheese—fold together with noodles using spoons.

Mark and Su Eikenberry
Will Rogers Park Personnel

"The man with a message is a whole lot harder to listen to."

Steak Soup

1 stick butter
1 cup flour
1/2 gallon water
1 pound ground beef
1 cup onions, cubed
1 cup carrots, cubed
1 cup celery, cubed
2 cups frozen mixed vegetables
1 can tomatoes
1 Tbls. monosodium glutamate
4 cubes beef bouillon
freshly ground black pepper

Melt butter and add flour to make a smooth paste. Stir in water; set aside.

Saute ground beef, drain grease and add to soup. Parboil the onions, carrots and celery. Add to the ground beef along with the mixed vegetables, tomatoes, monosodium glutamate, beef bouillon and pepper. Bring to a boil, reduce to simmer and cook until vegetables are tender. (Mrs. Alexander freezes this soup.)

Thank you for including the State of Tennessee in the celebration of Will Rogers' 100th birthday!

Lamar Alexander
Governor
State of Tennessee

Hamburger Pie

1 lb. Hamburger
1 small can tomato sauce
SAlt and Pepper (to taste)
1 medium can green beans
Potatoes-mashed (approx. 3)
1 onion (diced

Brown diced onions, add hamburger and brown. Stir in tomato sauce, salt and pepper. Place in casserole. Place green beans over meat mixture. Put potatoes over beans.

Bake in 350 degree oven about 30 minutes, or until mixture is bubbly. Variations to this recipe make it a different dish each time. Add the following: mushrooms to saute with meat mixture.

Cheeses, either cheddar or parmesan to the top of the potatoes or sour cream to the meat mixture when placing it in the casserole.

Add a salad, and you have a complete meal.

Jim and Gloria Stout
Pacific Palisades 1979
Citizens of the year.

"More's" One Dish Dinner

1-1/2 lbs. of ground round steak
1 package frozen peas *or* 1 can
1 can whole kernel corn
1-1/2 cups cooked shell macaroni
1 can tomatoes
1 can tomato sauce
1 Tbsp. chili powder

DICE:
2 onions
1 bell pepper
1 can mushrooms
2 small garlic buttons

Saute diced vegetables in small amount of salad oil, add ground meat, salt and pepper to taste, add chili powder. Add 1 can of tomatoes, 1 can tomato sauce. Let simmer for a while, then add peas, corn and cooked macaroni. Empty into a large Pyrex bowl and put cheese on top.

Mrs. William P. Clements, Jr.
First Lady of State of Texas

Currant Chicken

6-7 whole chicken breasts, split
2-8 oz. jars currant jelly
2 Tbls. cornstarch, dissolved in 1 cup cold water (shake in empty jar)
2 tsp. ground allspice
1/2 cup lemon juice
2 Tbls. Worcestershire
3 Tbls. Butter
3 Tbls. chili sauce
3 tsp. salt
1 tsp. pepper

Mix ingredients together to make sauce. Bring to a boil and simmer while stirring. Sauce can be stored for days in refrigerator until ready to use, or frozen. To bake chicken, lay out pieces so they don't overlap too much. Pour sauce over. Don't worry if sauce looks pale and thin. As chicken bakes it becomes dark and thick. Bake at 450 degree for 15 minutes. Reduce to 350 degree. Bake at least 1 hour, basting frequently. If sauce becomes too thick during baking, add water freely.

Serve with wild rice, or wild rice mixed with "ALA" or plain rice. Serve sauce separately.

Vivian Braun
Pacific Palisades Citizen of the year,
1970

Roast Duck with Sausage Stuffing

ROAST DUCK

Night before: Wash ducks thoroughly and place in a glass dish. Stuff each cavity with a celery stalk, 1/4 apple, 1/4 onion, a dash of poultry seasoning and a dash of thyme. Rub outside with salt and seasoned pepper. Pour (at least) a cup of your favorite wine over them, tightly cover, and let marinade overnight in the refrigerator.

Next morning, empty birds (save celery etc.). Stuff with sausage dressing and place in baking pan. Pour all the marinade, including celery, apple etc., over ducks and cook as you would a small baked hen, basting as you go, 350 degrees.

SAUSAGE STUFFING:

Prepare 2 pkg. of Pepperidge Farm herb dressing according to directions. Add one lb. of your favorite sausage (crumbled and well-browned). Add 2 c. chopped celery, 1 c. chopped pecans, 1 c. chopped onions.

This is a favorite recipe of Governor James.

Mrs. Fob James, Junior
The Executive Mansion
Montgomery, Alabama

Souffle de Saumon

Serves 4
Cook in 6-cup souffle mold
1 tsp. butter
2 Tb. plus grated Parmesan cheese
Butter mold and sprinkle with cheese. Preheat oven to 400 degrees.

2 Tb. minced green onions or shallots
3 Tb. butter
3 Tb. flour
1 cup milk (or juice from canned salmon and milk)
1/2 tsp. salt
1/8 tsp. pepper
1 Tb. tomato paste
1/2 tsp. oregano

Cook onions in butter for a moment. Add flour and cook over medium heat for 2 minutes. Remove from heat, beat in liquid all at once, then add seasonings and tomato paste. Boil, stirring, for 1 minute and remove from heat.

4 egg yolks
3/4 cup or more shredded cooked or canned salmon (Oregon Salmon, of course!)
1/2 cup grated Swiss cheese

With pan off of heat, beat in egg yolks one at a time, then add salmon and all but 1 Tb. cheese. Taste for seasoning.

Glaze with milk or melted butter, or cover surface with plastic wrap. Heat, stirring, to just warm before continuing.

5 egg whites
1/4 tsp. cream of tartar
pinch of salt

Beat egg whites slowly until they foam, then add cream of tartar and salt. Increase speed gradually and beat until stiff but not dry. Stir one-fourth of egg whites into sauce mixture. Gently *fold* in the rest. Pour into prepared mold and sprinkle with remaining cheese.

Bake in middle level of oven which has been preheated to 400 degrees. Turn oven down to 375 degrees and bake for 30-35 minutes. Check and bake 4-5 minutes after it is golden brown. Souffle is done when skewer comes out clean. Serve *immediately*. Will hold in turned off oven, with door open, for 5 minutes without collapsing.

NOTE: Before baking, souffle may be placed on doubled towel and covered with an inverted large pot for 1 hour.

Victor Atiyeh
Governor
State of Oregon

Patio—Will Rogers
Santa Monic

Casseroles

Spinach Ring

Cook 4 boxes of frozen chopped spinach and drain well. Further chop the spinach in a food processor, or put through a meat grinder. Beat together 4 eggs and 2 egg yolks and add the spinach.

In a sauce pan melt 4 T butter. Remove the pan from the fire, and stir in 4 T. flour. Return the pan to the fire, and gradually add 1-1/2 c. milk, salt, pepper, and nutmeg to taste. Fill a greased 1-1/4 quart ring mold, and cover the ring with greased waxed paper. Place the ring mold in another pan of hot water. Bake in a 350 oven for about 30 minutes, or until a knife comes out clean when inserted into the spinach. Remove from the oven and from the water, and allow to stand for a couple of minutes before unmolding. The center may be filled with other vegetables.

Harriet L Axelrad
Docent—Will Rogers State Park

Will went on a diet of spinach, broiled lamb chops and milk for three days every time he would come home from a trip to lose the weight he would put on.

Mr. Emil Sandmeier
former employee of Will Rogers

"Nothing thickens one like travel."

Arizona Enchiladas

1-1/3 c. enchilada sauce (recipe follows)
8 tortillas
3/4 lbs. ground round steak
1/2 tsp. salt
dash pepper
dash garlic salt
1/2 c. chopped onions
1/2 c. grated cheese
3/4 c. chopped lettuce
1/2 c. sliced ripe olives

Brown meat in skillet. Season with salt, pepper, and garlic salt. Heat enchilada sauce. While sauce simmers dip tortillas in sauce one at a time until softened. Remove and fill each tortilla with approximately 2 Tbs. meat, 1 tsp. lettuce, 2 tsp. cheese, 1-1/2 tsp. onion, and 2 tsp. olives. Roll and secure with a toothpick. Arrange tortillas in a greased baking dish, seam side down. Pour remaining sauce over top. Bake at 350 degrees for 25 minutes. Remove from oven and sprinkle with cheese. Bake 5 minutes more.

ENCHILADA SAUCE
1 can tomato soup-undiluted
1/4 tsp. garlic salt or 1 garlic bud
1/4 tsp. cayenne pepper
1/4 c. water
1/8 tsp. Oregano
dash salt

Combine all ingredients and simmer 10 minutes.

Donna Nolan
Docent—Will Rogers State Park

"We may elevate ourselves but we should never reach so high that we would ever forget those who helped us get there."

Mandarin Drumsticks

12 chicken wings
1/2 c. cornstarch
1 egg-slightly beaten
1/4 tsp. salt and 1/4 tsp. seasoned salt
2 Tbs. milk

Cut chicken wings at joint, discard wing tips. Scrape and push meat to one end of the bone, so each piece resembles a small drumstick. In a medium bowl, combine cornstarch, egg, salt, seasoned salt, and milk. Mix well until smooth. Dip each drumstick in batter. Drop in hot grease in a deep freyer or a mini-freyer. Fry until lightly brown. Drain well on paper towel. Place in single layers in a shallow baking pan. Bake at 350 degrees for 30 min. or until chicken is done. Add spicy glaze to chicken and sprinkle with sesame seeds to taste. Return to oven 10 min. Serve hot.

SPICY GLAZE
1 c. granulated sugar
1/4 c water
1/2 c. vinegar
1 tsp. soy sauce
1 Tbsp. catsup
1 Tbsp. chopped green onions (use tops too)

In a small saucepan combine all ingredients. Bring to a boil, stirring until the sugar dissolves.

Donna Raymond
Docent—Will Rogers State Park

"People's minds are changed through observation and not through argument."

Pork Chop Creole

6 thick pork chops (butterfly cut)
3/4 cup chopped onions
3/4 cup chopped celery
1 can tomato soup

Place chops in a flat casserole. Mix all other ingredients together and pour over chops. Cover and bake at 325 degrees for two hours.

Audrey McQuay

Vice-President
Docent—Will Rogers State Park

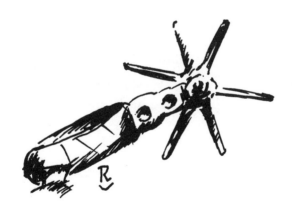

"We get into more things for less reason than any nation in the world."

Alettia's Sweet Potatoes

Layer 1
4 or 5 sweet potatoes baked, then mashed
2 T butter
2 T brown sugar
Mix together and spread into a casserole dish, sprayed with Pam.

Layer 2
8 oz. cream cheese at room temperature
2 T sour cream
Blend together, then spread on top of sweet potatoes

Layer 3
Brown on top of the stove.
2 T sugar
1/2 c graham crackers or vanilla wafers crushed
2 T butter
Sprinkle on top the cream cheese.

Garnish with pecan halves.

Bake at 350 degrees for 30 minutes.

Wes and Donna Howard
State Park Ranger

Noodle Pudding

Boil one half pound of flat noodles.

Wash noodles in cold water and drain.

Mix:
One 12 ounce package of sour cream,
One 8 ounce package of cream cheese (or cottage cheese)
1/4 pound of melted oleo or butter,
1/2 to 3/4 cup of sugar (to taste)

Add:
A dash of cinnamon
Six beaten egg yolks

After noodles have been added to above, fold in six beaten egg whites.

Bake in a greased loaf pan at 350 degrees, until firm. Serve hot. (This pudding can be reheated nicely.)

Variations:
Fold in canned fruit, or top with preserved cherries or blueberries or top with nuts and brown sugar or syrup. Great for brunch, lunch, or at a buffet!

Governor and Mrs. Milton J. Sharp
State of Pennsylvania

"Some men will stand for a lot of things. But you start taking their women or their jobs away from them and you are going to get something besides platitudes."

Ham Strata

6 slices bread
2 cups cooked, diced ham
1/2 cup chopped onion
1/2 cup chopped celery
1/2 cup green pepper
1/2 cup mayonnaise
1 cup milk
2 eggs
1 can mushroom soup
1 cup grated cheese
1 cup buttered bread cubes
salt and pepper to taste

Saute onion, celery, and green pepper until tender. Combine with diced ham.

Break bread into bite size pieces. Alternate layers of ham mixture and pieces of bread in buttered casserole.

Combine 2 eggs, beaten well, with 1 cup of milk and 1/2 cup mayonnaise. Pour over the casserole.

Refrigerate for several hours or overnight.

Before baking casserole, spread mushroom soup, plus buttered bread cubes, over the mixture and bake uncovered for one hour in 350 degree oven.

Remove from the oven and sprinkle top with a cup of grated cheese. Return to the oven until the cheese is melted.

Either chicken or turkey may be substituted for the ham in this one-dish meal. It may be made in the morning or night before and refrigerated until baking time.

Governor William G. Milliken
State of Michigan

112

Hamburger Casserole

1-1/2 lbs. hamburger
1/2 cup chopped onion
2 - 8 oz. cans tomato sauce
1 tsp. sugar
1 tsp. salt
1/4 tsp. garlic salt
1/4 tsp. pepper
8 oz. cream cheese
3 cups noodles
1 cup sour cream
1/3 cup green onion
1/4 cup chopped green pepper
Velveeta Cheese

In large skillet, cook meat and onion until meat is lightly brown and onion is tender. Stir in tomato sauce, salt, garlic salt and pepper. Remove from heat. Combine sour cream, cream cheese, green onion and green pepper. Cook noodles according to package and drain. Spead one-half noodles in baking dish, top with some meat mix, cover with cheese mix. Add rest of noodles and meat sauce; top with Velveeta cheese.

Bake at 350 degrees for 30 minutes. Makes 8-10 servings.

Governor and Mrs. J. James Exon
Nebraska

"When you get into trouble five thousand miles from home you've got to have been looking for it."

"Pure Oklahoma" Squaw Corn

4 slices bacon
1 green pepper chopped
1 onion chopped
1 can cream style corn
1 teaspoon salt
4 eggs, beaten

Fry bacon, set aside. Drain all drippings from skillet except 3 tablespoons. Cook and stir green pepper and onion in drippings until onion is tender. Add remaining ingredients. Cook and stir until eggs are thickened throughout, but still moist. Crumble bacon, sprinkle over egg mixture. Four to six servings.

Clem McSpadden
Great Nephew of Will Rogers

Corn and Oysters

1 can cream style corn
2 eggs
1/2 stick margarine
1 cup grated cheddar cheese
1 cup crackers
1 can oysters, drained

Mix corn, eggs, crackers and oysters together and pour into greased baking dish. Dot with margarine and spread grated cheese over top. Bake at 350 degrees about 30 minutes, until set.

Mrs. Clem (Donna) McSpadden
Chelsea, Oklahoma

"The best cure for temperament is hunger. I have never seen a poor temperamental person."

Farcis

(Stuffed vegetables)
Ingredients:
Minced ham
grated cheese
1 egg
1 boiled potato
1 onion
breadcrumbs
seasoning, and garlic to taste
round, ball squash
eggplants
large tomatoes

(Quantities depend on the number and size of vegetables to be stuffed)

Boil the squash and/or eggplants, but not the tomatoes, in salted water with the onion. When tender but still whole, drain and cut in half. Remove soft inside of vegetables and save. Mash up the boiled onion and mix with the ham and add crushed garlic if desired. Mash the potato and inside of vegetables and mix with ham, etc. Mix in some grated cheese. Bind together with beaten egg.

Now fill the squash and eggplants with this mixture, and raw tomatoes if used, from which inside has been removed. Top with cheese and breadcrumbs and cook in hot oven or under grill till brown.

Serve hot, or cold with salad.

Her Serene Highness
Princess Grace of Monaco

Zucchini Casserole

3 strips bacon
2-1/2 lbs. sliced zucchini squash
1/3 cup chopped celery
1/3 cup chopped onions
1/3 cup chopped green pepper
1 garlic clove minced
1 egg
Bread crumbs

Fry bacon, remove from pan. Saute onions, green pepper, celery, and garlic in bacon drippings until tender. Set aside.

Boil squash till tender, drain and mash well. Crumble bacon, add to squash. Add vegetables and the egg. Mix well together. Pour into a well buttered casserole dish. Line dish with bread crumbs (be generous). Pour in the mixture, top with bread crumbs. Dot with butter. Bake 30 minutes in a 400 degree oven or until top is crusty and brown. Let stand 10 minutes.

Claude Howard

Will Rogers Park

"Live your life so if you lose you are still ahead."

Chicken Enchilada Casserole

2 c. cubed chicken or turkey (cooked)
1 c. chicken broth
1 can cream of chicken soup
1 can (4 oz.) chopped green chilies
1/2 med. onion chopped
1 clove garlic, crushed
12 corn tortillas, cut into quarters
1 c. shredded monterey jack cheese
1 c. grated tillamook cheddar cheese
1 avocado and 3 cherry tomatoes for garnish

In med. bowl, mix chicken, broth, soup, green chilies, onion and garlic. Into a 1-1/2 qt. buttered baking dish, layer 1/3 of the tortillas, chicken mixture, jack and cheddar cheese. Repeat layers, ending with cheese on the top.
Bake at 375 degrees, 25 to 30 minutes. Meanwhile, slice avocado lengthwise, cut cherry tomatoes in halves, when casserole is done, arrange avocado slices spoke-fashion around top with tomato halves between.

Mrs. Gloria DeVries
Fresno, California

Mrs. DeVries knew Will in Oklahoma.

"We spoiled the best Territory in the World to make a State."

Creamed Tomato Cups

4 Med. size cucumbers
1 tsp. salt
6 Med. size tomatoes
1/4 cup of butter or margarine
1 cup heavy cream
pepper
2 tsp. chopped parsley
grated parmesan cheese

Pare cucumber, cut in half full length, scoop and seed, cut into 1/2 inch cubes, place in bowl and sprinkle with 1 tsp. salt. Toss a few times and let stand 1 hour, drain dry. Heat oven to 325 degrees. Slice tops of tomatoes, use spoon to scoop out pulp, seeds and juice. Sprinkle inside of tomato lightly with salt. Set aside. Melt butter or margarine in large skillet over medium heat. Add cucumbers and cook for 2 or 3 minutes tossing and stirring frequently, add cream and bring to a boil. Reduce heat and simmer 10 min. or until cream is reduced by half and cucumbers are tender. Season to taste. Remove the juice from tomatoes. Spoon cucumber mixture into tomato shells. Set in shallow baking dish. Sprinkle tops with parmesan cheese and bake 20 min. or until tomatoes are tender. Sprinkle with parsley. Makes 6 servings.

Bee Hodes
Docent—Will Rogers State Park

"Art is when you do something just cockeyed from what is the right way to do it."

Spaghetti Casserole

2 large onions chopped
1-1/2 lbs. lean ground beef
1-1/2 teaspoon salt or to taste
1 can Contadina Italian Sauce
1 small can sliced mushrooms
1 24 oz. can V-8 Vegetable juice
1/4 lb. spaghetti (or more)

Saute chopped onion until soft. Add meat and cook until pink color disappears. Add Italian Sauce, mushrooms and vegetable juice. Stir well. Cook slowly about 15 minutes. Add cooked and drained spaghetti. Stir well. Bake in greased casserole at 350 degrees for one hour. Serves 8.

Bea Heiby
Docent—Will Rogers State Park

Hominy Casserole (Mexican)

2 No. 2 cans hominy
1 c. scalded milk
1 c. bread crumbs
1 c. grated cheese
2 eggs, slightly beaten
1 Tbsp. butter
1 Tbsp. chopped green pepper
1 Tbsp. hot chili sauce
1 Tbsp. chili powder
1 Tbsp. grated onion
1 Tbsp. chopped parlsey
salt and pepper to taste

Mix all ingredients in order listed and place in buttered casserole, reserving some of the bread crumbs for topping. Bake in 350 degree oven for 40 minutes. Serves 4-6 people.

Mrs. DeVries and her father rode horseback with Will when she was a young girl in Oklahoma.

Gloria DeVries

"A man that don't love a horse, there is something the matter with him."

Broccoli Casserole

1/4 cup minced onions
1/4 cup butter
3 Tbsp. flour
1/2 cup water
3 eggs, well beaten
8 oz. Kraft or Velveeta pasteurized cheese-grated
2 10 oz. pkgs. frozen broccoli - chopped (cook & drain lightly)
1 lb. bacon - friend and crumbled

Saute onion in butter - stir in flour - and water and cook until thickened. Blend in cheese - add broccoli - fold in eggs. Pour into greased 1-1/2 quart casserole dish. Cover top with bacon - bake 45 minutes at 350 degrees. Serves 8.

Alice Sinniger
Office Assistant
Will Rogers State Historic Park

". . . you have to have a serious streak in you or you can't see the funny side of the other fellow."

Savory Sausage

2 lbs. bulk sausage
1 cup chopped green pepper
3/4 cup chopped onion
2-1/2 cups chopped celery
1 cup sliced blanched almonds
2 pkgs. Lipton's chicken noodle soup mix (with diced white chicken meat)
4-1/2 cups boiling water
1 cup Minute Rice
1 can water chestnuts chopped

Brown meat, pour off fat. Add green peppers, onion and celery. Saute. Combine soup mix and boiling water in large sauce pan. Stir in rice. Cover and simmer 20 minutes. Add rest of ingredients (sausage mix, almonds and water chestnuts). Stir well. Bake in greased casserole at 375 degrees for 30 minutes.

Serves 8 or 10.

Bea Heiby
Docent—Will Rogers State Park

Cheese Strata

12 slices bread (white preferred)
1/4 tsp. mustard (per slice)
1 lb. Wisconsin cheese, sliced (cheddar)
4 eggs beaten
2 c. milk
1/2 tsp. salt
1/4 tsp. pepper

Preheat oven to 350 degrees. Butter well a 9" x 13" pan. Place six slices of bread (spread with mustard) in pan. Add a layer of cheese. Repeat. Beat eggs well with milk Pour egg/milk mixture over bread and cheese. Season with salt and pepper. Bake 30 minutes. Cut in squares and serve warm, as an appetizer or snack.

Martin J. Schreiber

Martin J. Schreiber
Governor
State of Wisconsin

Scalloped Idaho Potato and Onion Casserole

3 lbs. potatoes
3 c thinly sliced onions
boiling water
3-1/2 tsp. salt
3 T. butter
2 T. chopped parsley
2 T. flour
1/2 tsp. paprika
1/2 tsp. pepper
2-1/4 c. milk

Preheat oven to 400 degrees. Lightly grease a 2 qt. casserole. Wash, peel and thinly slice potatoes, place in large sauce pan and add onions. Cover potatoes and onions with boiling water, add 2 tsp. salt. Cook covered 5 min., or until slightly tender, drain. Melt butter, stir in flour, paprika and rest of salt. Gradually stir in milk. Bring to boil, stirring, reduce heat and simmer one minute. Layer 1/3 potato and onion mixture. Sprinkle with 1 T parsley, top with 1/2 sauce. Repeat, ending with sauce. Bake uncovered 35 min. in mod. oven.

Governor John V. Evans
State of Idaho

Baked Beans

1 large can pork and beans
1 can green lima beans (drained)
1 can kidney beans (drained)
1 c celery (chopped)
1 c onion (chopped)
1/2 c brown sugar
1/2 c white sugar
1 lb. smoked ham

Mix all ingredients together and bake in a slow oven. 200 degrees - 250 degrees for 5 hours.

Governor John V. Evans
State of Idaho

Paula Stone Sloan (Fred Stone's daughter) laughed about Will. Her mother made some beans for him and apologized because they weren't the best but he said "there never was a bad bean."

"Barba Giuan", or Rissoles

1. Make short pastry with 250 grams flour, 100 grams margarine or butter, water, and salt.

2. Mince and boil Swiss chards.

3. Brown a minced onion in a saucepan, and mix with boiled Swiss chard, one egg, Parmesan cheese, salt and pepper.

4. Roll pastry into a thin sheet which you cut into round pieces (the size of a glass will do), and on the half of each round put a teaspoonful of the mixture. Then fold paste as in apple turn-overs, and seal with egg yolk.

5. Fry the rissoles in oil, and serve hot with tomato sauce.

Her Serene Highness
Princess Grace of Monaco

"My ancestors didn't come on the Mayflower, but they met the boat."

Lamb Chop Casserole

5-6 shoulder or rib chops
1 T flour
pepper
salt
5-6 slices of onion
5-6 slices of green pepper
1 can mushroom soup

Mix the salt, pepper, flour, and dredge the chops in the mixture.
Place chops in a casserole and top each one with a slice of onion and
green pepper.
Pour mushroom soup over everything and cover casserole.
Cook in a moderate oven from 1-1/2 to 2 hours.
Serve from the casserole if you wish.

Harriet Axelrad
Docent—Will Rogers State Park

Sherried Beef

2 lbs. stewing beef
2 cans cream of mushroom soup
2 T onion, minced
1 t black pepper
1 T Worcestershire sauce
1/2 pkg. dry onion soup mix
3/4 c Sauterne Wine

Cut beef into bite size cubes. Remove excess fat. Combine all
ingredients in a casserole and cook in a medium oven 350 degrees for
3 hours. Serve with rice. Serves 6.

Lisa Quarre
Aide—Will Rogers Park

Buddy Rogers' Eggplant Supreme

Slice an unpeeled eggplant into 1/2 inch thick slices.

Dip into salted tomato juice.

Roll in soy flour and place in layers in an oiled casserole.

Chop 2 cloves of garlic and 1 onion fine.

Mix with small can of cream style corn and one can solid tomatoes. Add salt

Pour mixture over eggplant.

Cover with grated Tillamook cheese, and bake in 350 degree oven for one hour.

Mary Pickford

Green Bean Casserole

2 lbs. string beans, fresh or frozen
1 can water chestnuts, drained and sliced
1 can bamboo shoots
2 cans mushroom soup
2 oz. grated cheddar or parmesan cheese

Layer all in buttered casserole, making two layers. Salt and pepper each. Bake 25 minutes at 400 degrees. Remove and sprinkle 1 can french fried onion rings over top. Put back in oven for 5 minutes. Serves 8.

Mrs. James B. Rogers (Astrea)

"The best way to judge just how good a man is, is to find out how he stands around his home and among his kind of people."

Quiche Lorraine

3 eggs, slightly beaten
2 cups light cream (half and half), or low-fat milk
1 cup shredded Swiss cheese
salt and pepper (1/4-1/8 tsp.)
1/2 cup chopped onion
1/2 cup melted margarine or butter
1/2 cup melted margarine or butter
1/2 cup crumbled cooked bacon
1 unbaked 9" deep pie shell
1 green pepper-chopped
1/2 cup chopped chives

Saute onion in butter (don't brown). Combine eggs, cream, cheese, salt and pepper, Add onion, butter, bacon, and green pepper. Pour into pie shell, and sprinkle with paprika. Bake at 400 degrees for 40 minutes

I have substituted low-fat milk for cream and margarine for butter to cut calories and it tastes the same.

Elyse Keane
Docent—Will Rogers State Park

Sweet Potato Casserole

3 cups cooked, mashed sweet potatoes
1 cup sugar
1 egg
1/2 t. salt
1/2 stick margarine
1 cup sweet milk
1/2 t. vanilla

Mix all ingredients with mixer and pour into 2 qt. casserole dish. Top with the following:
1 cup brown sugar
1/2 stick margarine
1 cup chopped pecans
1/2 cup flour
1/2 t. vanilla

Mix together and pour over sweet potato mixture. Bake at 350 degrees for 25 to 30 minutes. Serves 6 to 8 people.

Gov. Cliff French
Mississippi

131

All-Full Felafel

1 cup dry garbanzo beans cooked until soft
1/2 cup bulgar
8 large cloves garlic
2 tsp. ground cumin
1/2 cup lemon juice
1/2 cup wheat germ
1/2 cup chopped parlsey
1/4 tsp. cayenne pepper
2 eggs
1 tsp. paprika
2-4 Tbsp. wholewheat flour

Mash drained garbanzo beans by hand. Add the eggs and a few tablespoons of the lemon juice to the beans. Soak the bulgar in the rest of the lemon juice. Stir in the garlic, parsley and spices. Mix all other ingredients together. Add a small amount of flour to the mixture; if it falls apart when cooking add more. Form 2 inch wide patties and deep fry for 3-4 minutes at 375 degrees or cook thinner patties on an oiled skillet. Serve the felafel sizzling hot inside a split, warmed pita with sliced cucumbers, tomatoes, lettuce, pickles, alfalfa sprouts and sliced avocado. Top it with Tahini Sauce (available at any health foods store). Good eating!

Dan Jaffe and Christina Koegel
Will Rogers Park Aides

"I have always noticed that anytime a man cant come and settle with you without bringing his lawyer, why look out for him."

Italian Delight

1 small pkg. noodles, boiled in water
1 lb. hamburger, fried. Add 1 large onion, chopped
2 cloves garlic, minced
1/2 c green pepper
1 t parsley
a few pieces Rosemary
salt and pepper to taste

Next add 1 T Worcestershire sauce, 1/2 can whole kernel corn, 1/2 t tamale pie spice, 2 cans tomato hot sauce (or plain)
2 or 3 slices cheese cut small, and 1/2 t Grama's seasoning or chili powder.

Put in greased baking dish and bake 35 minutes.

Ron and Lee Elkins

Chief Ranger

Will Rogers State Park

"I never in my life made a single dollar without having to chew some gum for it."

Grandmother's Corn Pudding

Mix together:
2 T. flour
1/2 t. salt
1/4 cup sugar
Add:
1 can cream style corn (17 oz.)
1 can evaporated milk (5.3 oz.)
1/2 can of regular milk
3 slightly beaten eggs

Pour into a buttered casserole (1-1/2 qt. size). Sprinkle top with 2 tablespoons chopped butter. Place the casserole dish in a pan holding 1 inch of water. Bake at 400 degrees for 3/4 hour and check to see if center is firm. Sometimes it takes an hour.

Governor John N. Dalton
State of Virginia

Salads

Halved Avocados with Hot Cocktail Sauce

6 tablespoons butter or margarine
6 tablespoons catsup
2-1/2 tablespoons each vinegar and water
4 teaspoons sugar
2-1/2 teaspoons worcestershire
1/2 teaspoon salt
dash tabasco
4 small avocados
Shrimp, lobster or crabmeat

In the top of a double boiler, mix together the butter, catsup, vinegar, water, sugar, Worcestershire, salt and Tabasco to taste. Heat over boiling water until butter has melted and sauce is smooth. Cut avocados in half lengthwise, separate halves, and remove seeds. Add shrimp, lobster or crabmeat into hollow of avocado before covering liberally with hot sauce. Serve on a bed of lettuce leaves. Garnish with lemon wedge and serve as an appetizer. Makes 8 servings.

Footnote: Double recipe for sauce because you'll like it and wish you had made more. This particular sauce is great with any kind of whitefish. Will keep for weeks if refrigerated.

Mike O'Callaghan
Governor of Nevada

Calico Bean Salad

1 can (1 lb.) chick peas, drained and rinsed
1 can (1 lb.) kidney beans, drained and rinsed
1 cup chopped celery
1 cup chopped green pepper
1 cup cherry tomatoes, halved
Crisp iceberg and romaine lettuce leaves

Chili Dressing
1/2 cup tomato juice
1/2 cup vegetable oil
1/4 vinegar
1 envelope (1-2/4 ozs.) Chili seasoning

CHILI DRESSING
Combine tomato juice, vegetable oil, vinegar, chili seasoning. Stir or shake until well blended. Makes 6 servings, 1-1/3 cups dressing.

Combine chick peas, beans, celery, green pepper and tomatoes. Add enough Chili Dressing to moisten, and toss gently. Cover and refrigerate. Serve over greens.

Mr. & Mrs. Willard Cruse
Will Rogers Park Grounds Keeper

139

Cranberry Salad

1 lb. fresh cranberries
3 apples
1-1/2 c. sugar
2 oranges or 1/2 c. crushed pineapple
1/4 c. chopped walnuts
1 3 oz. Box cherry jello
2 c. hot water

Wash cranberries in cold water. Grind raw cranberries in food grinder. Pare and core apples and chop very fine. Add chopped oranges (or Pineapple), nuts and sugar. Dissolve gelatin in hot water. When cool add salad mixture. Pour into mold and allow to set.

Donna Raymond
Docent—Will Rogers State Park

Orange Jello Salad

2 pkgs. orange jello
1 cup hot water
1 pint orange sherbet
1 can mandarin oranges
1 small can Pet Milk, whipped
Pinch of sugar

Dissolve sherbet in water and jello.

Add whipped milk, oranges and sugar.

Chill and serve.

Mr. and Mrs. Willard Cruse
Will Rogers Park Groundskeeper

"What this country needs is more working men and fewer politicians."

Tapioca Salad

Soak 1 pkg. (large) tapioca in 4 cups water from 5-12 hours. Drain.

Cook in 2-1/4 cups milk on top of double boiler until soft (at least 30-45 min.).

Whip 1 cup cream and add 3/4 cup sugar. Drain 1 can fruit cocktail and cut up 1/2 jar maraschino cherries.

Cool tapicoa to luke warm and add cream (whipped) and the fruit. Stir well and chill.

Governor Harvey Wollman
State of South Dakota

24-Hour Layer Salad

Iceberg lettuce torn in bite-size pieces
1/2 green pepper, chopped
1/2 red pepper, chopped
1/2 cup celery, chopped
1/2 sweet red Spanish onion (other onions are too strong)
1 package frozen peas
1-1/2 cups mayonnaise
2 tablespoons sugar
4 ounces grated cheddar cheese
8 slices of crisp fried bacon, crumbled

Line a 13" x 9" x 2" pyrex dish with bite-size pieces of crisp iceberg lettuce. Sprinkle with chopped green pepper and chopped red pepper. If red pepper is not available, use the other half of the green pepper. Add a layer of chopped celery, then a layer of chopped sweet red Spanish onion, and a layer of uncooked frozen peas. Combine the sugar and mayonnaise. Spread over these ingredients. Sprinkle top with grated cheddar cheese. Top the salad with crumbled bacon. Refrigerate overnight.

Serves 10 to 12.

Robert F. Bennett
Governor-State of Kansas

Shrimp Salad

3 pounds cooked, chopped shrimp
6 hard boiled eggs chopped
chopped olives
1 cup chopped celery
juice of 3 lemons
salt and pepper
mayonnaise

To chopped shrimp add eggs, olives and celery; lemon juice, salt and pepper to taste and mayonnaise. Chill. Serves 9 to 12.

James B. Edwards
Governor-State of South Carolina

"Different" Salad

1 package thawed tiny peas
1/2 cup chopped onion
1/4 cup chopped celery
1/4 cup chopped crisp bacon
2 cups salted cashews
1/2 pint sour cream
salt and pepper

Mix peas, onions and celery in sour cream and refrigerate. Add bacon and nuts just before serving. Serves 4-6.

Jane Trinkkeller
Docent—Will Rogers State Park

Cucumber and Pineapple Salad

1/2 cup vinegar
Juice of 1 lemon
1/4 cup sugar
1/4 teaspoon salt
2 tablespoons gelatin (2 envelopes)
1/4 cup cold water
1 cup hot water
1 cup crushed pineapple
1 cup diced cucumbers (peeled)
  (use medium size cucumber)

Soak gelatin in cold water. Add hot water. Add vinegar, sugar and salt. Grease individual molds with Wesson Oil. When beginning to set, add pineapple and cucumber. Put into molds. Place in refrigerator. *Must cover with wax paper.* Makes 12-15.

Governor James B. Hunt, Jr.
State of North Carolina

Pungent Cabbage Slaw

4 c chopped cabbage
1/2 c chopped green pepper
Combine the chopped cabbage and green pepper.

Salad Dressing
1/2 t salt
2 T sugar
1 t celery seed
2 T tarragon vinegar
1 T prepared mustard
1/2 c salad dressing

Add seasoning to the salad dressing. Stir the dressing into the cabbage. Serve at once.

Optional: dill, caraway, parsley, beau monde, green onions.

Harriet L. Axelrad
Docent—Will Rogers State Park

Mexican Chef Salad

1 head lettuce
1/2 onion, chopped
4 tomatoes
4 oz. grated cheddar cheese
Toss all together

Add 8 oz. Thousand Island dressing, crunch and add one small bag Tortilla chips.

Slice and add one large avocado.

Brown one pound ground beef, add one 15 oz. can kidney beans (drained), 1/4 tsp salt. Simmer 10 minutes. Mix into cold salad.

Decorate with tortilla chips, avocado, and tomato slices. Serve immediately. 6 slices fresh mushrooms (optional).

Ron and Jan Jones
Ranger—Will Rogers State Park

"Americans are getting like a Ford car. They all have the same parts, the same upholstering and make exactly the same noises."

Spinach Salad

Serves 8

Large bunch of fresh spinach
2 hard boiled eggs, chopped
1 can water chestnuts—cut into pieces
6 strips of bacon—cooked, crumbled (use more if you wish)
1 can bean sprouts (if fresh, use 1/2 pound)
Mix together with dressing by tossing lightly.

DRESSING
1/2 cup white sugar
1/3 cup ketchup
1/4 cup vinegar
1/2 cup salad oil
2 tablespoons Worchestershire sauce
pinch of basil or lemon pepper

James R. Thompson
Governor, Illinois

24 Hour Slaw

1 medium head cabbage, shredded
1 medium onion, chopped
1 green pepper, chopped
12 stuffed olives, sliced

Mix all together and sprinkle 2/3 cup sugar over all. DO NOT STIR.

DRESSING
1 cup white vinegar
1 tsp. salt
1 tsp. prepared mustard
1 tsp. celery salt
pepper-to-taste
1/2 cup salad oil

Mix and boil three minutes, then pour immediately over slaw. DO NOT STIR. Cool, then cover and put in refrigerator 24 hours. Stir before serving.

Donna Nolan
Docent—Will Rogers State Park

"We are the first nation in the history of the world to go to the poorhouse in an automobile."

Marinated Bean Salad

1 can cut green beans
1 can wax beans
1 can kidney beans
1 can garbanzo beans
1 green pepper
1 bermuda onion

Slice green pepper and onion into thin rings. Combine with the four cans of drained beans.
Cover and marinade and refrigerate.

Marinade:
1/2 c sugar, scant
1/2 c red wine vinegar
salt
pepper
Combine in a saucepan, and stir over low heat until sugar dissolvss.
Add 1/2 c. salad oil. Mix well. Serves 6.

Audrey McQuay-Vice President
Docent—Will Rogers State Park

Avocado Ring

1 pkg. lemon flavored gelatin
1 c. boiling water
1 c. sour cream
1 c. mayonnaise
1 c. mashed avocado

Pour boiling water over gelatine and stir until dissolved—cool. Add sour cream, mayonnaise and avocado—turn into 8 inch ring mold which has been rinsed in cold water. Chill. Unmold and garnish with watercress, red grapes and unpeeled apple slices. Serves 8.

Helen McSpadden Eaton
(niece of Will Rogers)
Chelsea, Oklahoma

"I can't tell you where to write for I don't know where I will be."

Sauces

Barbecue Sauce

2 bottles catsup
1 bottle chili sauce
1/2 c mustard
1 T dry mustard
1-1/2 c brown sugar
1 t black pepper
1-1/2 T vinegar
1 c lemon juice
1/2 c steak sauce
Dash tabasco
1/4 t worcestershire sauce
1 T soy sauce
2 T salad oil
1 c beer
Garlic to taste

Cook on low heat for 1 hour or to desired thickness.

Karen Sapp
Docent—Will Rogers State Park

"No wonder American people are filling roads, trains, and air. There is so much to see. What we lack in reading, we make up in looking."

Lemon Sauce (for fish or vegetables)

2 egg yolks
2 Tbs. lemon juice (freshly squeezed)
2 Tbs. dill weed (not seed)
1 tsp. dry mustard
1/2 tsp. salt
1/2 tsp. each, thyme, m.s.g., lemon pepper, garlic powder, onion salt
(use any other herbs and seasonings you like)
1/2 cup salad oil
1/2 cup mayonnaise (low calorie is fine)

Blend eggs and seasoning well. Blend all ingredients with mayonnaise. Slowly pour in salad oil until all is smooth and blended. Spoon hot sauce over broiled fish or cooked vegetables.

Lynne Greditzer—President
Docent—Will Rogers State Park

"Presidents become great, but they have to be made Presidents first."

Jack Klugman's Spaghetti Sauce Recipe

1/3 cup olive oil
3 pounds pork with bone
1 pound sweet sausage
1 pound hot sausage
3 large cans whole tomatoes
2 large cans tomato puree
2/3 can water (whole tomato or puree sized can)
1 small can tomato paste (Contadina)
1 can water (small size of tomato paste can)
14 cloves pressed garlic
salt
pepper
fresh oregano
basil
parsley

Heat oil, add garlic, then brown. Add pork, sweet sausage, and hot sausage; brown. Put whole tomatoes, tomato puree, tomato paste and all water in blender; blend well. Add this tomato mixture and seasonings to meat and garlic, while stirring. Bring to a boil; place lid on and simmer for 2 hours, consistently stirring at least every 15 minutes.

Edith Cooper
Docent—Will Rogers State Park

"... anybody can open a Theater. It's keeping it open that is the hard thing."

Marinade Sauce

Sauce can either be used as a marinade or baste but is generally best as a baste. It can be used on poultry, pork, and beef. It adds that something special to a barbecue.

2 c water
1/4 c vinegar (wine)
1 can tomatoes (1 lb.)
1 can tomato paste (6 oz.)
1/2 lb. butter
1 clove garlic, minced
1 large onion, chopped
1/4 c lemon juice
2-1/2 t worcestershire sauce
2 t dry mustard
2 t ground black pepper
1/2 c tomato catsup
3 bay leaves
2 T sugar
2 t chili powder
1 can chopped green peppers, 6 oz.

Saute onion in butter until tender. Combine remaining ingredients and simmer in a covered pan for 30 to 45 minutes. Strain through a coarse sieve and cool. Sauce can be refrigerated several weeks until needed.

Jack Thompson
Maintenance Worker I
Will Rogers State Park

"I took my own fire and police protection with me. I wouldn't trust that Los Angeles bunch."

Spaghetti Sauce

1-1/2 pounds hamburger
3/4 tblsp minced onions
2-12 oz. cans tomato paste
1 pound can tomatoes
1-3/4 cups water
1-1/2 tsp oregano
1 tsp basil
1/4 tsp garlic powder
1 tblsp sugar
3/8 tsp salt
3/8 tsp pepper
1/2 cup chopped celery
1 bay leaf
pinch of red pepper

Brown the hamburger. Add the onions and cook until light brown. Add the remaining ingredients and simmer for one hour. Serves three to four.

Robert Elisberg
Aide—Will Rogers State Park

"The American people are generous and will forgive almost any weakness with the exception of stupidity."

Appetizers
and
Beverages

Avocado Dip

2 Avocados, mashed
1 Lemon, squeezed
1/2 pint Sour Cream
Salsa
1 Large Tomato, diced
Grated Cheddar Cheese
Grated Jack Cheese

Layer all the above in order given, for the best dip ever.

Carl & Iris Wilson
Area Manager Will Rogers

Lillie Bennitt's Broiled Bacon Sandwiches

White or whole wheat bread
sliced bacon
(1 slice of bread makes 3 sandwiches)

Toast slices of bread on one side only Cook strips of bacon in oven until transparent. Cut each slice of toast in 3 pieces and top untoasted side with 1/2 strip of precooked bacon. Place on cookie sheet and broil lightly. Serve immediately. These bacon sandwiches were served at the Will Rogers' Ranch house at outdoor gatherings.

Lillie Bennitt was a cook for the Rogers.

Caviar on Rye Rounds

Put a slice of hard-boiled egg on rye round. Cover with Caviar and add a little chopped onion and lemon juice.

Harriet L. Axelrad
Docent—Will Rogers State Park

Pea Pod Appetizer

Wash and string 24 Chinese pea pods and put in strainer. Pour boiling water over pods and allow to drain. With a small knife, make a slit in top of pod opposite peas.

1 8 oz. package cream cheese, softened
1 t. finely chopped fresh ginger
6 pimiento olives, chopped
1/2 c. roasted chopped almonds

Mix ingredients and put in pastry bag. Pipe pastry bag into slit in pea pod. Chill before serving. May be made the day before serving.

Harriet L. Axelrad
Docent—Will Rogers State Park

Tomato Juice Cocktail

1 peck ripe tomatoes
1 large onion
2 buttons garlic
1/4 cup vinegar
2 tablespoons salt
1 tablespoon celery salt
4 dashes Tabasco sauce
1/2 teaspoon salycilic acid

Method: Wash and quarter tomatoes, cook without adding water until well done. Add onion and garlic just before removing from fire and rub through colander. Put in kettle again adding remaining ingredients. Heat to boiling point and seal in sterilized jars.

Maude Rogers Lane
(Sister of Will Rogers)
Chelsea, Oklahoma

Company Hors D'oeuvres

3- 3 oz. pkg. cream cheese
5 pkgs. Alaska king crab (frozen or canned)
3 Tbls. hot horseradish
3 tbls. chopped chives
3/4 tsp. salt
Tabasco sauce to taste

Soften cream cheese with 3 tbls. of milk. Add balance of ingredients. Mix well. Put in oven dish and sprinkle with almonds. Bake at 400 degrees for 20 min. Serve piping hot, with Triscuits.

Edith Cooper
Docent—Will Rogers State Park

Irish Coffee O'Callaghan Style

Freshly ground coffee, fairly strong
One jigger Irish whiskey per cup of coffee

Top each serving with sweet whipped cream and grated chocolate if desired. Serve in heavy pre-warmed mugs.

Governor Mike O'Callaghan
State of Nevada

"Canada is a mighty good neighbor and a mighty good customer. That's a combination that is hard to beat."

"Plains Special" Cheese Ring

1 pound grated sharp cheese
1 cup finely chopped nuts
1 cup mayonnaise
1 small onion, finely grated
Black pepper
Dash cayenne
Strawberry preserves, optional

Combine all ingredients except preserves, season to taste with pepper; Mix well and place in a 5 or 6 cup lightly greased ringmold. Refrigerate until firm for several hours or overnight.
To serve, unmold, and if desired, fill center with strawberry preserves, or serve plain with crackers.

> With best wishes,
> President & Mrs. Jimmy Carter
> The White House

"*Plains Special*" Cheese Ring

1 pound grated sharp cheese   Black pepper
1 cup finely chopped nuts   Dash cayenne
1 cup mayonnaise   Strawberry preserves, optional
1 small onion, finely grated

Combine all ingredients except preserves, season to taste with pepper; Mix well and place in a 5 or 6 cup lightly greased ring mold. Refrigerate until firm for several hours or overnight.
To serve, unmold, and if desired, fill center with strawberry preserves, or serve plain with crackers.

With best wishes, *Rosalynn Carter*

"*No matter what a President does, he is wrong according to some people. . . .*"

Pickles Like My Zadie Used to Make

Remember the good-old fashion kosher dill pickles from the deli pickle barrel? Hot and spicy! Every year my grandfather would visit from Chicago and prepare for us large quantities of Jewish delicacies, and lots of mouth-watering pickles.

The recipe is easy to follow and requires no cooking or pressure sealing.

Ingredients Needed
quart size Mason canning jars with lids
kosher salt
pickling spices
jalpeno peppers (dry)
Fresh Dill
clove of garlic
fresh cucumbers (1-1-1/2" dia. & 4-5" long)

Begin by sterilizing the jars and lids. Wash the cucumbers in cold water. Dice plenty of garlic, and lay out the rest of the ingredients for easy access.

For each quart jar:
— Pack 4-5 firm cucumber upright in the bottom of the jar.
— Add one tablespoon pickling spice.
— Add two stems leafy dill down the sides.
— For the zesty flavor add 1-3 dry peppers. (The more peppers—the more flavor.)
— Add a generous pinch of diced garlic
— Top with 1-1/2 tablespoons kosher salt.
— Add 2-3 more cucumbers lying down across the top.
— Fill with cold tap water leaving about 1/2" of space at the top for expansion.

Hand tighten the lids and let stand over night. Store in a cool, dry place. In about 10 days you'll be ready to give your taste buds a treat.

(Note—Occasionally from expanding gases the lids may buckle. Simply loosen the lid, the gas escapes, then re-tighten.)

Chuck Bancroft
Ranger, Will Roger State Park

Pizza Things

---

1 small can chopped ripe olives
1/2 cup chopped green onions
1-1/2 cup sharp grated cheese
1/2 cup mayonnaise
1/2 tsp. each salt, chili powder and curry powder
6 English muffins, split

Mix all ingredients—spread on English muffins. Cut into quarters, bake 10 minutes, at 350 degrees. Then broil until bubbly.

Mrs. Betty Linton
1957 Citizen of the Year
Pacific Palisades

"There is dozens of great humanitarian things that could be done at a very little cost, if the tax was properly applied. It's the waste in government that gets everybody's goat."

Soups

Creme Sénégalaise

3 tablespoons butter
2 medium size green apples
2 stalks celery
2 medium size onions
2 teaspoons curry powder
2 teaspoons flour
1 quart chicken bouillon
salt
pepper
nutmeg
1 pint light craam (or evaporated milk)
1/2 cup white meat of chicken
paprika

Melt 3 tablespoons butter. Add two medium size green apples, peeled, cored and diced small; 2 stalks of celery finely chopped; and 2 medium size onions, grated. Cook until just beginning to take on yellowish color, stirring constantly; then sprinkle 2 teaspoons of curry powder (more if desired), mix with 2 teaspoons of flour. Continue cooking for 2 or 3 minutes longer, stirring constantly.

Gradually stir in 1 quart of chicken bouillon and bring to boil. Reduce the flame, and let simmer gently for 45 to 50 minutes. Empty the whole contents of the pan into a fine mesh sieve and rub through. Cool, after seasoning to taste with salt, pepper and a dash of nutmeg.

When cold, stir in 1 pint of liquid cream or undiluted evaporated milk and 1/2 cup of finely diced white meat of chicken.
Chill in refrigerator for 3 hours and serve in chilled soup plates, with garnish of sprinkling of paprika.

This is a cold chicken soup and one of our most favorite dishes.

Best wishes for the 100th birthday anniversary celebration of Will Rogers.

Evelle J. Younger
Former Attorney General
State of California

Bean Soup

3 slices bacon
2 c. baked or boiled beans
4 c. cold water
1 Tbsp. flour
1 Tbsp. butter
Salt, pepper, paprika (to taste)

Cook bacon, add to beans. Add water, cook until mushy. Press through strainer. Add a little water if needed. Beans should not be too thick. Thicken with flour and butter. Add seasonings to taste.

On one of the many visits to the Roger Ranch, Mrs. Stone saw Will walking around eating some beans with a shoehorn. She offered to get him a spoon. Will replied that he was doing just fine and went on eating.

Mrs. Fred Stone
(Given by Mrs. Paula Sloane, Fred
Stone's daughter)

Gumbo

1/2 Pound bacon
1/2 Cup chopped scallions & tops
2 Large onions
1 Large clove garlic (minced)
1 Bell pepper (minced)
4-5 Tablespoons plain flour
5 Cups water
2 Teaspoons salt
1 Teaspoons dried thyme
1/4 Teaspoon coarse ground black pepper
2 (1 lb. cans) tomatoes and liquid
2 Bay leaves
2 Tablespoons fresh parsley
2 Packages frozen okra
2 Cups diced ham
1 Teaspoon creole seasoning (optional)
3 Drops Tabasco
2 Pounds cooked shelled shrimp
1 Pound fresh or frozen crab meat
1 Teaspoon gumbo file powder (optional)

In a large soup kettle or Dutch oven, saute bacon until crisp; remove bacon, crumble and reserve. In bacon drippings, saute onions, scallions, garlic and bell pepper. Add flour. Brown to make "roux". Gradually add water, salt, thyme, pepper, tomatoes, bay leaves and parsley. Cover pot and simmer slowly for two hours. Add okra, diced ham, creole seasoning and Tabasco and simmer 15 minutes. Add shrimp and crab meat and simmer uncovered 10 minutes. Just before serving, add one tablespoon file powder. Spoon hot fluffy rice in serving bowls. Ladle gumbo over rice. Sprinkle with bacon bits and serve.

Georgia's coastal waters furnish a delicious bounty. Shrimp, crab and salt water fish are caught in abundance the year round.

Reservoirs, ponds and streams offer bass, trout and pan fish. The State is rapidly becoming a leading producer of catfish on a commercial basis.

Governor and Mrs. George Bushu
State of Georgia

Corn Chowder

1 stick butter
2 cups onions chopped fine
4 cups corn (cream style)
1 cup green peppers (chopped fine)
—if you like peppers—
2 cups milk
1 cup whipping cream

Saute onions and butter together. Add cream style corn and milk and cream. Add salt and seasoning—salt to taste. (add green peppers if desired).

Governor James A. Rhodes
State of Ohio

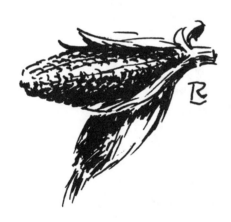

"Don't sell America short. Get some good stock and hold it till it's worth more, then sell, but don't gamble."

Hamburger Minestrone Soup

1 lb. ground beef
1 cup fresh onions, chopped fine
1 cup potatoes, chopped small
1 cup carrots, chopped small
1/2 cup celery, chopped small
1/2 cup cabbage, chopped small
No. 2 can tomatoes
1/4 cup rice
1 bay leaf
1/2 tsp. thyme leaves
1/4 tsp. basil leaves
5 tsp. salt
1/2 tsp. pepper
1-1/2 qts. water

Brown beef and onions. Add potatoes, carrots, celery, cabbage, tomatoes, rice and seasonings. Then add water. cover and simmer for 1 hour. Sprinkle with cheddar or parmesan cheese. Serves 5.

Mrs. James B. Rogers (Astrea)

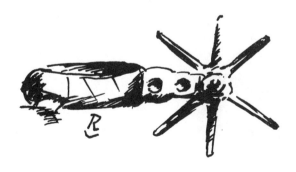

Clam Chowder

Several quarts of clams or quahogs
2 cups of water (broth)
1/4 lb. butter
1-3/4 cups thinly sliced onions
2 tbsp. flour
2-1/2 cups potatoes cut into 1/2" cubes
2 cups celery, coarsely chopped
1 bay leaf, quartered
2-1/2 tsp. salt
1/2 tsp. Accent
1/4 tsp. pepper
4 cups milk
1 cup medium cream
1 cup sour cream

Saute onions in 5 tsps. butter approximately five minutes. Remove from heat. Add flour and mix. Gradually add broth. Add potatoes, celery, seasonings and most of clams. Simmer until potatoes are tender.
Scald milk, remove from heat. Add cream and sour cream. Beat with beater until smooth. Reheat slowly (don't boil). Add to potato mixture with rest of clams. Heat fives minutes. Remove bay leaf pieces and top with remaining butter.

I am enclosing a copy of my favorite recipe for clam chowder which I hope you will enjoy as much as I do.

Michael S. Dukakis
State of Massachusetts

Boating Soup

1 3 ounce package cream cheese
1 small container no flavor yogurt
1 egg
1 can onion soup
2 cans bouillon soup or bouillon cubes added to water
salt and pepper
chopped parsley
nutmeg

Soften cream cheese. Beat it, yogurt and egg to a smooth paste. Bring soups to a boil, stir in yogurt mix OFF THE FIRE and stir until smooth. Put in individual bowls. Add dash nutmeg, sprinkle with parsley. May be served hot or cold.

Nini Holmes Lyddy
Docent—Will Rogers State Park

"When there is no malice in your heart there can be none shown in your homes."

Bay Country Crab Soup

1 pound beef shin, bone-in
3 quarts water
1 large onion, chopped
2 large stalks celery, chopped
1 1-pound can tomatoes
1 tablespoon salt
1/4 teaspoon black pepper
1/8 teaspoon cayenne pepper
1 10-ounce package frozen mixed vegetables
1 package fresh or frozen mixed soup vegetables
1 pound Maryland regular crabmeat
1/2 pound Maryland claw crabmeat

Put first 8 ingredients in a large pan and simmer, covered, until meat is very tender, about 3 hours. Add rest of ingredients and simmer, covered, until vegetables are done. Makes about 5 quarts soup.

Harry Hughes
Governor, Maryland

Breads

Basic Sourdough Recipe

2 Cups Sourdough Starter
2 Tbsp. sugar
4 Tbsp. oil
1 Egg
1/2 Tsp. salt
1 Scant tsp, soda; full tsp, if starter is real sour.

Into the Sourdough dump sugar, egg and oil. Mix well. Add soda the last thing when ready for batter to hit the griddle. Dilute soda in 1 tbsp. of warm water. Fold gently into Sourdough. *Do not beat.* Notice deep hollow tone as Sourdough fills with bubbles and doubles bulk. Bake on hot griddle to seal brown. Serve on hot plate.

Governor Jay S. Hammond
State of Alaska

"This Alaska is a great country."

Hot Water Cornbread

1-1/2 c. white cornmeal
1/2 Tsp. salt
3/4 c. boiling water

Bacon grease for frying, (oil or other shortening can be used). Mix cornmeal and salt in a pan with handle for holding. Pour in boiling water gradually beating constantly. When smooth, shape into flat pones. Fry in about one inch deep grease until lightly browned and crisp. Makes 8-12 pones.

Thelma Bacon
Member of the Pocahontas Womans
Club of Claremore, Oklahoma

Squaw Bread

2 c. flour
1 tsp. sugar
1/2 tsp. salt
1 c. milk
4 tsp. baking powder

Mix and roll like biscuits. Cut in 2x4 inch pieces and slit center. Fry in deep fat until golden brown.

Gladys Bell
Member of the Pocahontas Womans
Club of Claremore, Oklahoma

Zucchini Date/Nut Bread

2 cups pecans
4 eggs
2 cups brown sugar
1 cup vegetable oil
2-1/2 cups whole wheat flour
1 cup white flour
1-1/2 tsp. baking soda
1/2 tsp. nutmeg
1 tsp. cinnamon
3/4 tsp. baking powder
2 cups grated zucchini
1 cup dates
1 tsp. vanilla

Beat eggs, add sugar, then oil. Combine all dry ingredients and add to first mixture. Add squash. Stir in vanilla.
Grease 2 pans (9 x 5 x 2 inch).

Bake 350 degrees for 1-1/4 hrs. (or till done). Let stand for 10 minutes. Turn out on racks to cool. Serves 12.

Lew Ayres

Mr. Ayres made State Fair with Will Rogers in 1933.

"No matter how late you are, you are never too late for pictures."

Leola's Cornbread

1-1/2 cups buttermilk
1/2 teaspoon soda stirred into milk
1 egg
2 Teaspoons baking powder
1 teaspoon salt
1 teaspoon sugar
3 tablspoons bacon drippings
3/4 cup meal

Melt drippings in skillet and when it is hot, pour in mixture.

Beat till smooth.

Bake at 450 degrees until done and brown. (About 20 minutes or a little more depending on the shape of the pan.)

Note: If the sheet of batter is thin, it doesn't take as long as a thick layer in a smaller pan.

Governor David Pryor
State of Arkansas

Fayetteville, Ark., Feb. 22.--
"Say, if you want to visit the most beautiful country in the United States, don't overlook these Ozark Mountains. In these are where I grabbed off my only wife. So you will pardon me for bragging on Arkansas.

Florida Orange Bread

3/4 cup Florida orange rind (about 4 oranges)
1-1/2 cups sugar
1/3 cup water
3 tablespoons butter
1-1/2 cups orange juice
3 eggs well beaten
4 cups sifted all-purpose flour
4 teaspoons baking powder
1/2 teaspoon soda
1 teaspoon salt

Remove the thin orange rind with a sharp knife, cutting around the orange; cut rind into very thin slivers with scissors or knife. Combine sugar and water; add rind; stir constantly over heat until sugar is dissolved; cook slowly 5 minutes. (The peel and syrup should measure 1-1/3 cups).

Add butter, stir until melted; add orange juice and beaten eggs. Sift together into mixing bowl—flour, baking powder, soda and salt. Add orange mixture and mix just enough to moisten ingredients (batter should be lumpy). Bake in greased and lined loaf pan 9x5x3" in slow oven (325 degrees) 1 hour and 15 minutes. Turn out on rack to cool. Yield—1 loaf.

Governor Reubin Askew
State of Florida

"The higher up our officials get, the less they seem to know about human nature."

Self-Rising Bread

3 c self-rising Flour (Gold Medal)
2 T sugar
1 12 oz. can Beer at room temperature
Melted Butter, to top the loaf

Mix together dry ingredients. Add beer 1/3 at a time. Mix well. Pour into a well greased pan. Dribble butter over the bread. Half way through the baking, dribble more butter. Bake 1 hour at 350 degrees. Makes 1 loaf pan 9x4x3, 2 medium small, or 3 small pans.

Mary Olivera
Docent—Will Rogers State Park

"A bunch of American tourists were hissed and stoned yesterday in France but not until they had finished buying."

Bread

Mix 1 package active dry yeast in 1-1/4 cup very warm water.
Add:
2 T shortening
2 T sugar
2 t salt
1-1/2 c flour (I use unbleached.)

Mix with beater until smooth, scraping the sides with a spoon. Add 1-1/2 cups flour (I use 3/4 c wheat) and mix with spoon. Cover and let rise until double.

Beat down with spoon and stir. Pour into loaf pan, flour hands and pat down top. Cover and let rise until even with top of pan. Bake at 350 degrees for about 35-40 minutes. Remove from pan and place on top while hot. Let cool.

Ron & Jan Jones
Ranger—Will Rogers State Park

"The first political party that is far-sighted enough to buy airplanes instead of votes is going to be setting mighty pretty the next few years."

Corn Bread

1 cup sifted all purpose flour
1 cup corn meal
2 Tablespoons Sugar
4 teaspoons baking powder
1 teaspoon salt
2 eggs, slightly beaten
1 cup milk
1/4 cup shortening, melted

Sift flour with corn meal, sugar, baking powder and salt into mixing bowl. Combine eggs, milk and shortening. Make a well in center of dry ingredients. Add liquid ingredients all at once; stir until smooth. Pour into greased 8" or 9" square pan. Bake at 425 degrees for 20 to 25 minutes, until golden brown. Cut into squares; serve immediately.

Karen Sue Sapp
Docent—Will Rogers State Park

"They (his doctors) wouldn't let me have any chili, but I got the next best thing that I wanted, and that was some real cornbread."

Spoon Bread

2-1/2 cups milk
3/4 cup corn meal
2 Tablespoons butter
3 eggs, separated
1/4 cup all purpose flour
1 teaspoon salt
1 teaspoon baking powder

Combine 1-1/2 cups milk and corn meal in saucepan. Cook, stirring constantly until mixture comes to a boil. Remove from heat. Stir in butter. Add remaining milk, egg yolks, flour, salt and baking powder; mix well. Beat egg whites until soft peaks form. Fold into batter. Pour into a well-greased 2-quart casserole. Bake at 375 degrees for 35 to 45 minutes, until golden brown. Serve immediately.

Karen Sue Sapp
Docent—Will Rogers State Park

Will Rogers Centennial Celebration Corn Bread

1 cup yellow corn meal
1 cup flour
1 Tablespoon baking powder
1 teaspoon salt
1/3 cup soft butter
1 large egg (or two small)
1 cup milk

Combine all dry ingredients, mix well. Add butter, blend well. Add egg and milk. Mix all together until just blended. Pour into well buttered 8" square pan. Bake in hot oven (400 degrees) 25 minutes.

Donna Raymond
Docent—Will Rogers State Park

"Old words is like old friends, you know 'em the minute you see 'em."

Corn Meal Pancakes

1 cup flour (sifted)
1/2 cup corn meal
2-1/2 teaspoons baking powder
1/2 teaspoon salt
2 eggs
1 cup milk
2 Tablespoons shortening (fresh bacon fat is good)

Separate eggs; beat whites until stiff but not dry. Sift dry ingredients together; stir egg yolks into milk and add to egg whites, then stir in dry ingredients and shortening. Mix only enough to blend. Drop on a moderately hot griddle (375 degrees) and turn once when pancakes are bubbly on top. Serve immediately with butter and New Hampshire maple syrup.

I am honored to be included in this project and pleased to enclose a recipe that is often served at our Mt. Cube Farm in Oxford, New Hampshire.

I am looking forward to visiting the Will Rogers State Historic Park.

Meldrim Thomson, Jr.
Governor—State of New Hampshire

192

Desserts

Banana Cake

2-1/4 cups sugar
3/4 cup Wesson oil
3 eggs
2-1/2 cups flour
6 tablespoon buttermilk
1-1/2 teaspoons soda
4 large bananas (mashed)
1-1/2 teaspoons vanilla

Cream sugar, oil and egg yolks. Add bananas, buttermilk, and flour. Last, add egg whites (beaten stiff). Makes a big cake. Pour into greased pan and bake at 350 degrees for 35 to 45 minutes. GREAT!

Mrs. Clem (Donna) McSpadden
Chelsea, Oklahoma

Claremore, Okla., June 20. "Say, what do you know about Claremore having a golf course? I tell you turning your land into a golf course is the salvation of the farmer. That's the only thing to do with land now, is just to play golf on it."

Moose Meat Mince Meat

1 pound moose meat
1/2 pound beef suet
4 apples
1 quince
3/4 pound sugar
1/2 cup molasses
1 pint cider
1 pound seeded raisins
3/4 pound currants
1 tbls. finely cut citron
1/2 pint cooking brandy
1 tsp. cinnamon
1 tsp. mace
1tsp. nutmeg
1 tsp. cloves
1/4 tsp. pepper
Salt to taste

Cover meat and suet with boiling water and cook until tender. Cool in water in which cooked. When cool remove layer of fat. Then finely chop meat and suet and add to it twice the amount of finely chopped apples, the quince finely chopped, sugar, molasses, cider, raisins, currants, and citron. Reduce stock in which meat and suet were cooked to 1-1/2 cups, and add to the fruit and meat mixture. Heat gradually, stirring occasionally, and cook slowly 2 hours (in thrift cooker). Add brandy and spices.

This can be put in jars while boiling hot and sealed for future use. This recipe makes 7 or 8 pints. Use as for any mince meat pie.

Governor Jay S. Hammond
State of Alaska

New Hampshire Wild Blueberry Pie

Spread over bottom of cooled, baked 9" pie shell—1 package of cream cheese (3 oz.) which has been softened. On top of this pour one pint of the largest and best blueberries—not cooked. Mash one pint of blueberries and add water, if necessary, to make 1-1/2 cups. Bring to a boil and gradually stir in mixture of 1 cup sugar and 3 Tblsp. of cornstarch. Cook over low heat, stirring constantly until boiling. Boil one minute. Cool. Pour over the berries in pie shell. Chill about 2 hours. Just before serving, decorate with whipped cream. Wild blueberries make the best pie but cultivated berries may be used.

Governor Meldrim Thompson, Jr.
State of New Hampshire

"There is as many gadgets on the market to overhaul men as there is women. I doubt if women have got much on men when it comes to trying to outlook themselves."

Hope's Lemon Pie

8" pie shell, baked
1 cup sugar plus 2 Tblsp.
3 Tblsp. cornstarch
1 cup boiling water
4 Tblsp. lemon juice
2 Tblsp. butter
4 egg yolks (save the whites)
Pinch of salt
Grated rind of (1) lemon

Combine the corn starch and sugar; add the water slowly, stirring constantly until thick and smooth. Remove from heat. Add the slightly beaten egg yolk, butter and lemon rind and juice and salt. Cook, stirring constantly, for 2-3 minutes. Cool. Pour into baked pie shell.

Top pie with a meringue made from the (3) egg whites, beaten stiff with two and a half teaspoons of sugar. Bake at 350 degrees for 15 minutes, or until lightly browned.

Bob Hope

Bob Hope a master chef? Hardly. With his current schedule, he can only enjoy—not participate—in the cuisine. However, a great weakness of his is lemon pie. Here is the way his mother used to make it.

"It's great to be great, but it's greater to be human."

Mabel's Perfect Piecrust

4 c flour
1 T sugar
2 t salt
1-3/4 c shortening
1 T white or cider vinegar
1 large egg

1. Put first 3 ingredients in large bowl and mix with a fork.

2. Add shortening mix until crumbly.

3. In a small bowl beat with a fork, 1/2 c water, the vinegar and egg.

4. Combine the two mixtures, stir until moistened.

5. Divide dough in 5 portions and shape each into a flat round patty ready for rolling.

6. Wrap in wax paper then enclose in ziplock bag for freezing.

7. If you plan to use the same day chill at least 1/2 hour before using.

8. When ready, flour both sides of patty, place between two pieces of wax paper then roll it to desired size.

Makes two 9" double and 1 single shell or 20 tart shells. If making cream pie bake shell at 475 degrees for 8 to 10 minutes.

MABEL'S PECAN PIE FILLING
3 eggs beat until ropey
Add 1/2 c Karo and 1/2 c maple syrup or 1 c Karo
1/2 c sugar

Mix well then add 1 c whole pecans, 1 t vanilla. Bake in pie shell at 350 degrees for 40 minutes.

Wes and Donna Howard
State Park Ranger

Southern Pecan Pie

8-inch unbaked pastry shell
3 eggs
1 cup dark corn syrup
1/4 cup sugar
1 Tablespoon flour
1 teaspoon vanilla extract
1 cup coarsely chopped pecans

Combine eggs, corn syrup, sugar, flour and vanilla extract in mixing bowl. Beat until well blended. Add pecans. Pour into 8-inch pastry-lined pan. Garnish with pecan halves, if desired. Bake at 350 degrees for 35 to 45 minutes, until center is firm to the touch.

Karen Sue Sapp
Docent—Will Rogers State Park

"You can look at half the guys' stomachs in the world, and you can see they don't know how to order for themselves."

Buttermilk Pie

1-1/2 c. sugar
2-1/2 Tbsp. flour
1/4 tsp. salt
In another bowl, mix:
3 eggs (beaten)
5/8 c. buttermilk, beat together and add
4 tbsp. melted butter
1/2 tsp. lemon juice
1/2 tsp. vanilla
1/2 c. coconut (angel flake)

Mix together with dry ingredients and pour into unbaked pie shell. Bake at 425 degrees until it starts to brown and reduce heat to 300 degrees for 45 minutes.

This was a typical farm recipe in Oklahoma when I was a child.

Gloria DeVries

Aunt Lib's Doughnuts

1 large cake yeast
1 cup lukewarm milk
2 eggs, beaten
1/2 stick butter
1/8 tsp. salt
1/4 cup sugar
Grated rind of 2 lemons
1/2 tsp. nutmeg

Crumble yeast in 1/2 cup of lukewarm water. Add 1 Tbsp. sugar, set aside for 10 minutes. Place lukewarm milk and beaten eggs in bowl. Add yeast. Add enough flour to make a soft sponge (about 1-1/2 cups). Let raise in warm place until double in bulk. When raised, add butter, salt, sugar, grated lemon rind and nutmeg. Knead in enough flour for a soft dough. Let raise again. Roll to 1/2" thickness. Cut with doughnut cutter. Place doughnuts on a floured board. Cover with towel and let raise until double in bulk. Fry in hot grease until golden brown. Roll in granulated sugar.

Donna Raymond
Docent—Will Rogers State Park

"Now if there is one thing that we do worse than any other nation, it is try and manage somebody else's affairs."

Granola Snack

1/2 cup granola, the brand of your choice
2 tablespoons soy bean nuts, salted (dry roasted) (45 percent protein)
1 tablespoon sunflower seeds
1 teaspoon roasted sesame seeds
1 teaspoon wheat germ
1 tablespoon raisins, with no preservatives added
1 cup nonfat milk, either fresh or powdered
Add fresh fruit to taste. Serving for one.

This recipe makes a superb, tasty satisfying meal for breakfast, lunch or dinner. It is nutritious and good for your head and all interior plumbing systems. It leaves you light and full of energy.

Marvin Braude
Los Angeles City Councilman

"I'll bet you the time ain't far off when a woman won't know any more than a man."

Impossible Pie

Beat thoroughly—4 eggs
Add
1/4 c. melted butter
1-1/2 c. sugar
1/2 c. flour
3/4 tsp. baking powder
2 c. milk

Beat together until well blended, stir in 4 ozs. shredded coconut. Pour filling into two ungreased deep, 8 inch pie plates and bake at 350 degrees, 40 minutes, or until brown on top. Cool in refrigerator.

Robert Elisberg
Aide—Will Rogers State Park

"The short memories of American voters is what keeps our politicians in office."

English Trifle

1 package yellow or pineapple layer cake mix (18.5 oz.)
1/2 cup raspberry jam
1/2 cup sherry or 1/3 cup orange juice, plus 2 tablespoons sherry flavoring
1 can vanilla ready-to-serve pudding (18 oz.) or make your own
1 cup chilled whipping cream
1/2 cup sugar
1/4 cup toasted slivered almonds—candied cherries, chopped

Bake cake in oblong pan, 13" x 9" x 2", as directed on package. Cool. Cut cake crosswise in half. Reserve one half for future use. Cut remaining half into 4 squares. Split each square, fill with 2 tablespoons jam. Arrange squares in 2 quart glass serving bowl, cutting squares to fit shape of bowl. Pour wine over cake and allow to soak into the cake a few minutes. Spread with pudding. Chill at least 8 hours. In chilled bowl, beat cream and sugar until stiff. Spead over trifle. Sprinkle with almonds and cherries.

Variation: Strawberry Trifle
Substitute 1 package frozen strawberry halves (16 ounces), thawed, for the raspberry jam. Omit sherry and do not fill cake squares. Arrange half the cake in bowl, top with half the strawberries and spread about 1/2 cup pudding over berries. Repeat. Chill at least 8 hours. In chilled bowl, beat cream and sugar until stiff, spread over trifle. Sprinkle with almonds and cherries. Serves 10 to 12.

Robert F. Bennett
State of Kansas

Cranberry Crunch

1 cup quick cooking oatmeal
1/2 cup all purpose flour
1 cup brown sugar, firmly packed
1 stick margarine
1 (1 lb.) can whole cranberry sauce

Mix oatmeal, flour and brown sugar together. Cut in stick of margarine until mixture is crumbly. Pack 1/2 of this mixture into greased 8" x 8" pan. Cover with whole cranberry sauce. Top with remaining crumb mixture. Bake at 375 degrees for 45 minutes. Serve warm, topped with vanilla ice cream.

Governor James B. Longley
State of Maine

Carrot-Pineapple Cake

2 cups grated carrots
2 cups sugar
1-1/2 cups vegetable oil

Combine and beat ingredients; add 4 eggs, one at a time, beating well after each addition. Sift 2 cups flour with 2 teaspoons soda, 1 teaspoon salt, and 1 teaspoon cinnamon. Add to first mixture. Add 1 small can crushed pineapple, including juice. Bake in three eight-inch layer pans greased, lined with waxed paper, then greased and floured. Bake in a pre-heated 350 degree oven about 35 minutes.

ICING
1 8-ounce package cream cheese
1 stick butter
Cream ingredients together and add 1 one-pound box powdered sugar, 1 teaspoon vanilla, and 1/2 cup nuts. Ice cake between layers only.

Governor David L Boren
State of Oklahoma

"Leaving the glorious State of Oklahoma tonight by popular demand."

Maggie Cake

1 cup butter
2-1/2 cups sugar
5 eggs, beaten separately
1 cup buttermilk
5 teaspoons coffee
2 teaspoons vanilla
3 cups flour
1 teaspoon baking powder
1 teaspoon soda
4 teaspoons cocoa
1 teaspoon salt

Mix ingredients. Add stiffly beaten egg whites last. Makes five layers.

ICING
1 pound powdered sugar
3 teaspoons coffee
1 egg
1/2 cup butter
2 teaspoons cocoa
1 teaspoon vanilla
dash of salt

Put all ingredients into mixing bowl except sugar. Start mixing, gradually adding sugar, and cream if needed, to make right consistency for spreading. Icing is good when chocked full of Oklahoma pecans.

This recipe is named for Mrs. Maggie Prather of Stratford, Oklahoma, who is a life-long friend of the A. H. Shi Family. The Shis are the parents of Mrs. Molly Shi Boren, First Lady of Oklahoma.

Governor David L. Boren
State of Oklahoma

Oma Cake

Ingredients:
1-1/2 cups sugar
3/4 cups shortening
2 1-oz squares chocolate
2 eggs
2 cups flour
1 tsp. baking soda
1 tsp. cinnamon
1 scant tsp. salt
1 cup buttermilk or sour milk
2 tbsps. lemon juice

Cream sugar and shortening thoroughly. Add 1 egg, beat one minute. add another egg, beat one minute. Melt 2 1-oz. chocolate squares and cool. Mix together flour, baking soda, cinnamon and salt. Mix alternatively with milk. Add cool chocolate with lemon juice. Bake at 325 degrees for 25 minutes.

Filling:
2 egg yolks, 1/2 cup sugar, 1 tsp. vanilla, 1 cup milk, 3 tsp. flour
Beat egg. Add sugar, flour. Add milk slowly—cook in double boiler until it thickens. Add vanilla.

Icing:
Beat 2 egg whites stiff. Add 3/4 cup confectioners sugar. In another bowl mix to smooth cream 1 cup confectioners sugar and 4 tbsp. butter. Add 2 squares melted chocolate. Combine with stiff egg white and sugar. Mix and beat until nice, smooth, thick taste.

Oma Cake is one of the Governor's favorite recipes from his mother's collection.

Governor Richard A. Snelling
State of Vermont

"You people certainly have a wonderful country in this America, . . ."

Buttermilk Pound Cake

Cream together:
1 cup butter (soft)
3 cups sugar
Add 5 eggs, one at a time, and beat 10 minutes.
1-1/2 tsp. vanilla
3 cups flour
1/2 tsp. each soda and salt.
Sift together, add alternately with 1 cup buttermilk. Bake in tube pan 1-1/2 hr. at 325 degrees. Test with straw or cake tester before removing from oven.

I am pleased to be asked to submit a recipe for the Will Rogers Cookbook. I will never forget the day Will Rogers died. I was living on a ranch in Texas. I felt like I'd lost a friend.

Dorothy Larson
Citizen of the year 1959
Pacific Palisades

"You must judge a man's greatness by how much he will be missed."

Virginia Apple Cake

1 cup salad oil
2 cups sugar
2 eggs (large)
3 cups chopped Virginia apples (tart)
2 t. vanilla
1/2 t. cinnamon
1/2 t. nutmeg
3 cups flour
1 t. baking soda
1 t. salt
1/2 cup chopped nuts (or 1 cup chopped pecans)
1/2 cup raisins
3 T. sugar mixed with 1 tsp. cinnamon for coating pan

Combine sugar and cinnamon mixture. Grease tube or bundt pan and shake sugar-cinnamon mixture around in it until sides and bottom are well coated.

Mix oil with sugar in electric mixer until well mixed. Add eggs one at a time beating well after each addition. Sift flour, cinnamon, nutmeg, baking soda and salt. Add vanilla and mix well. Slowly add the sifted flour mixture. Add the apples, nuts and raisins. Pour batter into pan and bake at 325 degrees for 1-1/2 to 2 hours. Usuaully 1-3/4 hours is about right. (Better is unusually thick.)

Governor John N. Dalton
Commonwealth of Virginia

"Been traveling today down through the beautiful Shenandoah Valley of Virginia—and boobs are leaving to see Europe!"

213

Coconut Pound Cake

2 c. sugar
1 c. crisco
Cream together and add 5 eggs.
1 tsp. coconut flavoring
2 c. sifted flour
1-1/2 tsp. baking powder
1 c. buttermilk
1 tsp. salt
1 3-1/2 oz. package coconut

Mix all well together and put in a bundt pan. Bake one hour at 350 degrees.
Boil for one minute:
1 c. sugar
1/2 c. water
1 tsp. coconut flavoring
Pour over hot cake and let set 10 minutes, then remove from pan.

Ramona Wilt
President, Pocahontas Womans Club
Claremore, Oklahoma

"Claremore, Okla. is just waiting for a high-tension line so they can go ahead with locating an airport."

Chocolate Buttermilk Cake

1/2 c butter, 1/2 c brown sugar, 1/2 c white sugar
2 eggs
2 squares chocolate, melted
1 tsp. vanilla
2 c flour
1/2 tsp salt
1/2 c buttermilk
1 c boiling water, with 1 tsp. soda in it.

Cream butter and sugars together, add eggs and beat, add melted chocolate and vanilla, beat until smooth. Add sifted ingredients and buttermilk alternately. Boil 1 C water and add 1 tsp. soda. Mix together. Bake at 350 degrees—layer pan 30-35 min.; dripper pan, 40-45 min. Frost with chocolate frosting. This is a very moist cake.

Governor John V. Evans
State of Idaho

Tangerine Cheesecake

1 11 oz. box no-bake cheesecake mix
1/4 cup melted butter
2 Tbsp. sugar
1-1/2 cup milk
2 tangerines—peeled and cut in bite size pieces

Prepare graham cracker crust with butter and 2 Tbsp. sugar according to package directions. Chill.

Prepare cheese filling with milk according to package directions. Fold in tangerine pieces, spoon into crust.

TOPPING
1 Tbsp. fresh grated tangerine peel
1 cup dairy sour cream
2 Tbsp. sugar
Combine all topping ingredients well. Spread over filling. Garnish with one peeled tangerine in segments. Chill. Serves 8.

Donna Raymond
Docent—Will Rogers State Park

Joanne's Milkyway Cake

8 milkyway bars
3 sticks of butter or margarine
4-1/2 cups sugar
4 eggs—beaten
2-1/2 cups flour
1/2 teaspoon baking soda
1-1/4 cups buttermilk
1 cup chopped pecans
1 small can evaporated milk
1 6 oz. package chocolate chips
1 cup marshmallow creme

Combine candy bars and one stick of butter in a double boiler. Cook over low heat, stirring constantly, until melted. Set aside. Cream together 2 cups of sugar and 1 stick of butter in a bowl. Then beat in the eggs. Sift the flour and soda together and then add to creamed mixture alternately with buttermilk. Stir in candy mixture. Add pecans and mix well. Pour into a bundt pan. Bake at 325 degrees for 1 hour 10 minutes.

FROSTING
Combine remaining sugar (2-1/2 c.), evaporated milk and butter in a saucepan and cook to a soft boil stage (stirring frequently). Remove from heat and add chocolate chips and marshmallow creme. Cool slightly. Beat until thick and spread over cake. An oblong cake pan may also be used.

Karen Sue Sapp
Docent—Will Rogers State Park

". . . if your time is worth anything, travel by air. If not, you might just as well walk."

Oatmeal Cake

Place in a bowl:
1-1/4 cup boiling water
1 cup quick oatmeal
1 stick oleo
Cover and let stand 20 minutes
Then add:
1 cup white sugar
1 cup brown sugar
2 eggs
1-1/2 cups sifted flour
1 teaspoon soda
1 teaspon cinnamon
1 teaspoon salt
Mix well and bake in oblong pan for 35 min. at 350 degrees

TOPPING
2 tablespoons oleo
1/4 cup canned milk
1/2 cup sugar
1/2 cup coconut
1/2 cups chopped nuts
1/2 teaspoon vanilla

Mix in sauce pan till sugar is melted. Spread over hot cake and place under broiler until bubbly and slightly browned.

Will Rogers made his first radio broadcast over Pittsburgh's pioneer radio station KDKA in 1922.

Governor Milton J. Sharp
State of Pennsylvania

Wine Cake

1 package yellow cake mix
1 package vanilla instant pudding
4 eggs
1 tsp. nutmeg
3/4 cup oil
3/4 cup cream sherry

Mix ingredients together for 5 minutes. Pour into a greased and floured angel food cake pan (removable center type). Bake at 350 degrees for 50 minutes. When cooled, turn cake out of pan. Top with whipped cream when served, if you wish.

A sauce to pour over whipped cream may be made by creaming any type of canned fruit in a blender. A small amount of brandy may be added to the fruit if desired.

This cake is excellent for picnics, since it does not need a topping and may be preserved by wrapping in foil.

Governor Mike O'Callaghan
State of Nevada

Carrot Cake

2 cups sugar
1 cup salad oil (I use corn oil)
4 eggs
1 teaspon vanilla
Beat well. Add slowly mixture of dry ingredients:
2 cups plain flour
2 teaspoons baking powder
1/2 teaspoon salt
2 teaspoons soda
2 teaspoons cinnamon

Fold in 3 cups of grated carrots. Bake in three well greased and lined 8 inch pans for 25 minutes at 350 degrees.

Filling:
1 stick corn oil margarine
8 ounce package of cream cheese
1 box powdered sugar
1 cup chopped nuts
1 teaspoon vanilla
Let ingredients stand at room temperature before mixing. Mix and spread between layers and on top.

Governor James B. Hunt, Jr.
State of North Carolina

Wonder Cookies

1 cup peanut butter
1 cup pitted and chopped dates
1 cup chopped nuts
1 can Eagle brand condensed milk

Mix well and drop from spoon on cookie sheet and bake slowly.

Mary Pickford

Cornflake Cookies

Cream together:
1 cup soft butter or oleo
1 cup white sugar
1 tsp. vanilla
Add:
1-1/2 cups sifted flour
1 tsp. cream of tartar
1 tsp. baking soda

Stir in (by hand) 2 heaping cups fresh uncrushed corn flakes. Drop by 1/2 teaspoon onto cookie sheet. Bake 10 to 12 minutes at 350 degrees. Cool slightly before removing from pan. They brown as they cool. Makes about 5" dozen cookies.

Jane Trinkkeller
Docent—Will Rogers State Park

"If Lindy will come here I will show him Mary Pickford's home."

Sugar Surprises

3/4 cup butter
2 cups brown sugar
2 eggs beaten
1 cup flour
1 teaspon vanilla
3/4 cup nut meats
1 teaspoon baking powder

Cream butter and sugar, add other ingredients in order given. Pour into a 10 x 14 inch pan about 1 inch deep. Bake 20 to 30 minutes in a moderate oven. The batter will rise and then fall—the secret is to take it out as soon as it falls. Cut into any size squares or fingers that you like.

James B. Edwards
Governor—State of South Carolina

Matty's Anise Cookie

These are distinct in taste and will add to a cookie plate for Christmas Holidays.
Beat:
3 eggs at room temperature until thick and light
1 c sugar, add gradually and beat 20 minutes longer
Add:
1-1/3 c flour
1/2 t salt
1-1/2 t anise extract
Drop on greased and floured cookie sheet. Bake at 325 degrees. Let stand at room temperature about 8 hours.

Wes and Donna Howard
State Park Ranger

Oatmeal Drop Cookies

1-1/4 c sugar
1/2 c shortening
2 eggs
6 T (full) molasses
1-3/4 c flour
1 t soda
1 t salt
3/4 t cinnamon
2 c quick-cooking rolled oats
1/2 c chopped nuts
1 c seeded raisins

Cream together sugar, shortening, and eggs. Add molasses.
Gradually add dry ingredients, nuts, and raisins. Place on a greased
cookie sheet. Drop by teaspoonfuls onto cookie sheet. Bake 8 to 10
minutes, not until dry inside. 375 degrees.

Harriet Axelrad
Docent—Will Rogers State Park

*"Always excitement at a Democratic anything. There is always something
that will stir up an argument even if they all agree."*

Lemon Squares

1 cup Gold Medal flour
1/2 cup butter or margarine, softened
1/4 cup confectioners sugar
2 eggs
1 cup granulated sugar
1/2 tsp. baking powder
1/4 tsp. salt
2 tbsp. lemon juice

Heat oven to 350 degrees. Cream flour, butter and confectioners sugar. Press evenly in bottom of ungreased square pan, 9x9x2 or 8x8x2. Bake 20 minutes. Beat remaining ingredients until light and fluffy, about 3 minutes. Pour over hot crust and bake about 25 minutes longer or until no imprint remains when touched lightly in center. Cool and cut into 2" squares. Makes 16.

Chocolate Squares
Follow recipe for Lemon Squares except—decrease butter to 1/3 cup, omit lemon juice, and add 1 sq. (1 oz.) unsweetened chocolate, melted and cooled, to beaten egg mixture.

Governor Milton J. Shapp
State of Pennsylvania

Kit Cowdrey Cookies

(Created for our fourteen grandchildren)
2/3 cup shortening or margarine
1 cup flour
2-3 cups granola, natural cereal or oatmeal
3/4 teaspoon baking soda
1/4 teaspoon salt
1/4 teaspoon nutmeg
1 teaspoon cinnamon
3/4 cup brown sugar
1/4 cup honey
1 mashed banana
1-2 eggs (depending how moist one likes cookies)
1/2 cup walnuts
1/2 cup chocolate chips

Measure shortening into bowl, mix in honey, egg, brown sugar and banana. Sift flour, soda, salt, cinnamon and nutmeg. Gradually add to flour mixture while beating with electric beater. Stir in by hand the cereal (granola, oatmeal, etc.) Dough will be very stiff, can add a little vanilla or water to help. So each cookie will have nuts and chocolate chips, spoon dough on cookie sheet and press nuts and chips on each one. For a special treat, cookies can be frosted.

HONEY BUTTER FROSTING
1/4 cup butter
1/4 cup honey
2 cups confectioners sugar or less
1 teaspoon water or what it takes to have a just-right frosting
Blend honey and butter. Add water gradually to make a spreadable frosting.

Kit Cowdrey
Reporter—Santa Monica Evening Outlook

"A breakfast without a newspaper is like a horse without a saddle."

Fudgey Brownies

1/2 cup butter or oleo
4 sq. unsweetened chocolate
4 eggs
2 c. sugar
1 c sifted flour
1 tsp. vanilla
1 c. chopped nuts

Melt butter and chocolate over hot water; cool slightly. Beat eggs until foamy. Gradually add sugar, beating well after each addition. Add chocolate mixture and blend. Stir in flour, add vanilla and nuts. Spread in a greased and floured 9x9x2 inch pan. Bake at 325 degrees for 40 minutes; cool and cut in squares.

Ramona Henry Wilt
President of the Pocahontas Womans
Club of Claremore, Oklahoma

Will was a member of the Womens Club for a summer. He and a few of his boyfriends went in on a dare. Will was made an Honorary member. The club was organized on June 29, 1899.

Spider Cookies

1 12 oz. pkg. Butterscotch Bits
1 12 oz. pkg. Nestles Chocolate chips
1 c cocktail nuts
1 large pkg. Chinese Noodles

Melt Butterscotch Bits in double boiler, then melt chocolate chips. Add nuts and noodles. Mix well. Drop by spoonful onto waxpaper. Refrigerate 1/2 hour only. Makes 48 cookies.

Mary Olivera
Docent—Will Rogers State Park

English Toffee Cookies

1 cup butter or oleo
1 cup sugar
1 tsp. vanilla
1 egg (separated)
2 cups flour
1 tsp. cinnamon
1/2 tsp. salt
1 cup chopped walnuts

Cream butter and sugar till smooth. Add vanilla. Add egg yolk. Mix. Sift flour with cinnamon and salt. Blend with first mix. Spread evenly over greased pan (10 x 15 inches). Use back of spoon and palm of hand to spread.
Beat egg white slightly. Spread on top of dough to cover. Sprinkle nuts evenly on top. Press into dough. bake in slow oven 275 degrees about an hour, until brown. Cut into 1-1/2 inch squares while warm. Remove from pan later.

Jane Trinkkeller
Docent—Will Rogers State Park

Wild Grape Dumplings

Bring to a rolling boil one half gallon grape juice, sweetened with two cups sugar. Juice from possum grapes makes the best dumplings, but any grape juice may be used.

Make dumplings from one cup of water, two tablespoons melted shortening, one teaspoon baking powder and enough flour to make a stiff dough.

Roll out thin on floured board and cut into small pieces. Drop pieces one at a time into the boiling juice. Cook over high heat about five minutes, then simmer with the cover on about 10-12 minutes. Remove from heat and let stand 5-10 minutes before removing the lid. May be served with cream.

Sincerely,

Dr. Reba Collins, Curator

Will Rogers Memorial

Claremore, Oklahoma

Each year a Wild Onion dinner is sponsored by the Pocahontas Club of Rogers County and Claremore. This is an organization formed as a "pasttime" club by the girls of the area in 1899 and one to which Will Rogers and some of his young friends belonged at one time when they teased the girls into letting the boys join.

The dinner is a treat for anyone. The menu includes scrambled eggs cooked with wild onions; thick slices of ham; Indian style hominy; fry bread (sometimes called "squaw bread"), sassafras tea and wild grape dumplings.

Dr. Reba Collins wrote her doctoral thesis on Will Rogers and probably knows more about him than anyone else. She is a dedicated worker at the Will Rogers Memorial.

"I am just an old country boy in a big town trying to get along. I have been eating pretty regular and the reason I have is, I have stayed an old country boy."

Fresh Strawberry Trifle

Serves 8-10
2 box strawberries
1/4 c sugar
1 box vanilla pudding
1 angel food cake
1/2 c Marsala Wine
Cool Whip

Wash and slice strawberries, save a few for garnish. Marinate berries in 1/4 c Marsala. Make pudding according to package and cool slightly. Tear cake and place half in bottom of deep casserole, sprinkle 1/2 the remaining wine over the cake. Spread 1/2 the pudding over the cake, then 1/2 the berries with the juice. Repeat. Spread Cool whip over all and garnish with the berries. Refrigerate.

Audrey McQuay
Vice-President
Docent—Will Rogers State Park

"There is nothing as determined as a woman that carries on, and there is millions of 'em."

Cream Cheese Cupcakes

Makes six
Crust:
1/2 c graham crackers or vanilla wafers
1-1/2 T melted butter
Combine above ingredients and fill lined muffin cups.
Cream filling:
8 oz. cream cheese
1 egg
optional 1/2 t lemon rind grated fine
1/4 cup sugar
1 t vanilla

Dave and Elizabeth Nelson
State Park Ranger

"Washington, D.C. papers say, "Congress is deadlocked and can't act". I think that is the greatest blessing that could befall the country."

Pots de Creme

6 oz. chocolate chips
3/4 c. milk
1 egg
1/4 c. sugar
1 tsp. vanilla
dash of salt

Put chocolate chips, egg, sugar and salt into a blender. Heat the milk just to boiling and pour into the blender. Blend for 30 seconds, till all the chips are melted. Add the vanilla and 1/2 tblsp. of brandy or other liquor, if desired. Pour into small cups and refrigerate till firm. You may decorate them with nuts, whipped cream, shaved chocolate or a cherry.

Governor Richard D. Lamm
State of Colorado

Favorite Ice Cream

One quart buttermilk
One pint whipping cream
Two cups sugar
One tablespoon vanilla

Mix all ingredients and pour into ice cream churn and freeze.

This is Gov. Edward's grandmother's recipe.

Governor James B. Edwards
State of South Carolina

No Bake Sweet Treat

1 pkg. 6 ounce semi sweet chocolate pieces
1 pkg. 6 ounce butterscotch pieces
3/4 cup sifted confectioners sugar
1/2 cup dairy sour cream
1 tsp. grated orange rind
1/2 tsp salt
1-3/4 cups crushed chow mein noodles
3/4 cup ground walnuts
1 small pkg. coconuts

Melt chocolate and butterscotch pieces together over hot water in double boiler. Remove from heat add remaining ingredients except nuts. Mix well. Chill dough 20 minutes. Shape into 1 inch balls. Roll in ground walnuts. Store in tightly covered container. Makes about 3-1/2 doz.

Bee Hodes
Docent—Will Rogers State Park

"All we have to do to get in bad is just to start out on what we think is a good samaritan mission."

Chocolate Ice Box Dessert

Ingredients:
chocolate chips
sugar
water
eggs
whipping cream
vanilla
salt
angelfood cake

Method:
Line flat 9x9 cake pan with wax paper. Slice angelfood cake and place a layer of cake in cake pan. (I find that angelfood cake slices better if frozen.) Separate six (6) eggs, beat egg yolks. Melt one (1) twelve ounce package of chocolate chips in a double boiler or over water, when melted add four (4) tablespoons of sugar and six (6) tablespoons of tap water, mix well, be sure sugar melts.

Remove from heat and stir the above hot chocolate mixture gradually into the beaten yolks of eggs, beat until smooth. Cool chocolate mixture. Add two (2) teaspoons of vanilla and one teaspoon salt, mix. Beat the six (6) egg whites until stiff; whip two (2) cups of whipping cream. Fold egg whites into the cooled chocolate mixture, then the whipping cream. Place a layer of the chocolate mixture on the sliced angelfood cake, then another layer of cake, then a layer of chocolate. Place in refrigerator and chill overnight. This may be frozen and used later. Be sure to chill overnight before freezing.

Gerald R. Ford

President and Mrs. Gerald R. Ford

Cornell's Ice Cream

4 baskets (one quart) of fruit (blackberries, strawberries, apricots or peaches)
1 cup of sugar
juice of 1 lemon
1 quart of half and half.

Mix in blender. Chill. Turn in icea cream maker. Makes one gallon.

Elinor Oswald
Pacific Palisades,
"L.A. Today"

Pumpkin Pudding

2 cans prepared pie mix (Libby's) that will make 2 9" pies
1/2 lb. butter
1 spice cake mix
2 T cinnamon

Follow instruction for making pies on back of cans. Add cake mix and cinnamon, mix well. Pour into a greased 9x11x2 glass baking dish. Melt butter and pour over the top of pudding. Bake in 325 degree oven 35-45 minutes. When pudding is done the knife will come out clean. At the edge of the dish a pool of butter will remain. Serve hot or cold with whipped cream.

Carl & Iris Wilson
Area Manager,
Will Rogers State Park

"Hollywood Bowl is located between Hollywood and Beverly, the Sodom and Gomorrah of the Orange Juice Belt"

Lemon Squares

1-1/2 cups flour
3/4 cup of butter
Cut butter into flour like pie crust. Pat down in baking pan, (9x11).
Bake 10 minutes at 350 degrees till light brown.

Filling:
1 cup brown sugar
1-1/2 cups coconut (shredded)
1 cup chopped nuts
2 eggs beaten
1/4 tsp. baking powder
1/2 tsp. vanilla
Mix together and spread on above crust. Bake 20 minutes, 350 degrees until light brown. Let cool, then ice with:

Icing:
1 cup powdered sugar
1 tblsp butter (melted)
Juice and rind (grated) of one lemon
Cream together and spread over the above. Cut in 2 inch squares.

Nelda Lockwood
Park Aide, Will Rogers Park

Hazel's Float

This is a recipe our family makes for anyone not feeling well. It helps to pick you up! No one seems to turn it down.

3 c milk, heat in a pan
2-3 eggs separated, beat yolks and add
1/2 c sugar
3 T Flour (rounded). Add a little hot milk, then mix all with milk and eggs. Cook a few minutes until it thickens.
Add a pinch of salt
1/2 t vanilla

Beat egg whites until stiff.

Pour milk and egg mixture over beaten egg whites, then fold in gently. Sprinkle with nutmeg.

Optional:
Add sliced bananas, oranges, pineapple, or whatever.

Sally Gessford
Docent—Will Rogers State Park

238

Butch's Favorite Cookies

Cream together:
3/4 c white sugar
3/4 c brown sugar
1 c shortening
2 eggs
Add dry ingredients:
2 c flour, mix into the above
1 c oatmeal
1 c chopped nuts
1/2 c coconut
1/2 c chocolate chips, or carob

Mix this all together. Drop by spoonful onto a ungreased cookie sheet. Bake at 375 degrees for 12-15 minutes.

Wes & Donna Howard
Ranger, Will Rogers State Park

Forgotten Cherry Torte

Torte:
Preheat oven to 450 degrees
4 egg whites
1/4 tsp. salt
1/4 tsp. cream of tartar
1 cup sugar
1/4 tsp. almond extract

Beat egg whites until frothy; sift salt and cream of tartar over whites and beat to form soft peaks. Gradually add sugar, beating until dissolved and very stiff peaks form. Add almond extract.

Draw 8 inch circle on heavy paper (brown paper bag works well), place on cookie sheet. Spread meringue 1/2 inch thick on circle, build up edges with remaining meringue. Place sheet in oven, close the door, turn off the gas and let remain in oven undisturbed overnight or at least 5 hours.

Filling:
1/2 cup sugar
2 Tbsp. cornstarch
Dash salt
2/3 cup cherry juice
1 Tbsp. butter
1/4 tsp. almond extract
1 can (1 lb.) pie cherries drained
Blend sugar, salt and corn starch—stir in cherry juice. Cook over medium heat, stirring constantly, until thick and clear. Mix in butter, cherries and almond extract. Chill. Spoon into torte shell several hours before serving.

Topping:
1 cup whipped cream
2 Tbsp. sugar
1/4 tsp. almond ext.

Add sugar and extract to whipped cream. Frost top of torte with cream; chill.
Serves 6-8

Alice Karl
Docent—Will Rogers State Park

Walnut Meringues

---

2 egg whites
1-1/2 teaspoons vanilla
1/4 teaspoon salt
2/3 cup sugar
2 teaspoons grated orange peel
2 cups walnuts cut in pieces

Preheat oven to 250 degrees. Combine egg whites, vanilla and salt. Beat with electric beater until foamy. Add sugar a tablespoon at a time, beating after each addition. Beat till soft peaks form and all sugar is dissolved. Fold in orange peel and walnuts.

Drop rounded teaspoons on cooky sheet covered with baking paper. Top with more walnuts, if desired.

Bake at 250 degrees till dry and a very light ivory color. Turn off oven and leave in 1 hour longer. Makes about 4 dozen cookies.

Ranger Gary McLaughlin
Will Rogers State Park

"No one is going to spoil the country but the people. No one man can do it and all the people are not going to do it, so its going to run in spite of all the mistakes that can happen to it."

Poppy Seed Cookies

2 eggs
1 cup sugar
1/2 cup oil
1/4 tsp. salt
Juice of one orange
1/4 cup poppy seeds (soaked in boiling water)
2 cups flour
2 tsp. baking powder

Soak poppy seeds in boiling water, let stand while mixing other ingredients. Beat eggs, sugar and oil together, add orange juice then flour, baking powder and salt. Put poppy seeds in strainer and rinse with cold water. Drain well. Add to batter and mix well. Roll small amount of batter at a time on floured board, using more flour as needed. Cut out with cookie cutters. Place on a lightly greased cookie pan. Bake at 350 degrees oven until light brown.

Edith Cooper
Docent—Will Rogers State Park

"You cant beat an administration by attacking it. You have to show some plan of improving it."

Gram's Cake

A hearty coffee cake to appeal to the true Will Rogers bean buff named in honor of the lovely lady who cooked her beans country style too.

2-1/2 c flour
1-1/2 c brown sugar
1/2 c butter or Margarine
1 t cinnamon

Mix all into crumbs, take out 1 cup for the top. Add 1 cup buttermilk.
1 t baking soda, dissolved in a little warm water. Stir and pour into greased 9" pan. Spread crumbs evenly on top. Bake at 350 degrees about 30 minutes or until cake tester comes out clean.

Dorothy Newton
Docent—Will Rogers State Park

"Shrewdness in Public life all over the World is always honored, while honesty in Public Men is generally attributed to Dumbness and is seldom rewarded."

Republican

1 c flour
1/2 c walnut
1/2 c butter

Mix. Press in foil lined 9x13 pan. Bake 5-8 minutes. Cool completely.

Beat 8 oz. cream cheese and 1 c powdered sugar till light. Fold in 1 large cool whip. Spread on cooled crust.

Mix 2 small Instant Fudge pudding with 2-1/2 c milk. Pour over cream cheese layer.

Spread 1 small cool whip on pudding layer.
This can be frozen overnight, then lift out by foil, and sliced.

Ron and Jan Jones

Ranger, Will Rogers Park

"I'd rather be right than Republican."

Lorie's Grasshopper Dessert

Beat 1/2 pint whipping cream until stiff. Blend in 1 pint soft vanilla ice cream. Add 2 T green cream de menthe, and 2 T white cream de cocoa. Add a few drop green food color. Pour into sherbert glasses. Freeze until firm.

Variations:
Pink Squirrel
Substitute 1/4 cup cream de cocoa and 1/2 t almond flavoring for cream de menthe and cream de cocoa in grasshopper recipe. Add a few drops red food coloring instead of green.

Brandy Alexander
Substitute 2 T Brandy and 2 T cream de cocoa for cream de menthe and cream de cocoa in grasshopper recipe.

John Falk
Will Rogers Park Aide

"I never saw an audience that I ever faced with any confidence."

245

Hasty Cake

Sift together:
1 cup sugar
1 cup flour
1/2 tsp. salt
1 tsp. baking powder

Melt in a measuring cup about 1/3 cup butter. When cool drop in one large or two small eggs and fill cup up with milk.

Add one teaspoon vanilla and mix *well* the dry and liquid ingreidents. Bake in about 400 degree oven until the cake springs back when touched with finger, about 20 minutes.

BUBBLE CAKE
Spread the following topping over the hasty cake when you take it from the oven, and then put it under the broiler very briefly until it begins to bubble and brown lightly.

To 1 cup brown sugar add about 1 tespoon of flour, some broken nut meats, some coconut if you have it, vanilla and cream enough to make it spread easily.

I am happy to offer the following, which was a favorite of my grandmother's and is much admired by all her descendants.

Robert Abernethy
1972—Citizen of the Year
Pacific Palisades
NBC television—Washington, D.C.

Ozark Pudding

1 egg and 3/4 cup of sugar, beaten for a long time until very smooth.
Add to egg-sugar mixture: 2 tablespoons of flour, 1-1/2 teaspoon
baking powder, and 1/4 teaspoon salt.
Fold in: 1/2 cup of chopped raw apple
1/3 cup of chopped nut meats
1 teaspoon vanilla

Bake at 350 degrees in a well greased pie plate for 30 to 35 minutes.
Serve with whipped cream or ice cream. A little rum adds to the
taste.

Apparently this will fall but that is correct.

Bess Truman

Mrs. Harry S. (Bess) Truman

Peach Ice Cream

Make a boiled custard of 1 quart cream, 1 pint milk, 3 eggs, 1 cup
sugar. To this, when cool, add 1/2 gallon of soft peaches mashed and
well sweetened. This makes one gallon of ice cream which is most
delicious.

With our Stonewall peaches this makes our very favorite "company
dessert"—a summer treat without equal.

Mrs. Lyndon B. Johnson

Lady Bird Johnson

247

Della's Persimmon Pudding

1-1/2 c sugar
2 c flour
2 t soda
1/2 t nutmeg
1/2 t cinnamon
1 c nuts
1 c raisins
1 c persimmon pulp
1 egg
1/2 c oil

Mix all dry ingredients together. Mix all the wet ingredients together. Now mix the two together. Stir in nuts and raisins. Bake in a covered pan or tin. I use a 1 lb. coffee tin with a tinfoil lid. Fill the tins only half full.

Place tins in a pan of water so to steam the pudding. Bake at 375 degrees for 2-1/2 hours. When cool cut the bottom from the tin, and push the bread out, then wrap in tin foil to store or save.

Mark and Su Eikenberry
State Park Ranger

Aunt Freda's Peanut Butter Cookies

2 cups flour
3/4 Tsp. baking soda
1/2 Tsp. baking powder
1/4 Tsp. salt
1/2 cup butter
1/2 cup peanut butter
1/2 cup brown sugar
1/2 cup granulated sugar
1 egg
1/4 cup orange juice

Mix all well together. Roll in a ball, the size of a walnut. Put on a lightly greased cookie sheet. Press ball down with a fork dipped in granulated sugar. Bake in 350 degree oven—10 to 12 minutes. Cookie is soft and keeps well.

Donna Raymond
Docent—Will Rogers State Park

"Be a politician; no training necessary."

Plum Pudding

1 quart seeded raisins
1 pint currants
1 pint finely cut citron
1 quart finely cut apples
1 quart finely cut suet
1 heaping quart bread crumbs
1 quart juice (grape etc.)
8 beaten eggs
1 pint sugar
nutmeg, cinnamon spices to taste

Method:
Enough flour to make a stiff dough added to the above as given.
Steam four hours. This makes four nice puddings. Reheat by steaming
one when wanted, and serve with hard sauce made as follows:
Cream 1/2 pound of butter, gradually adding 3/4 pound powdered
sugar, stirring and beating until like whipped cream. Flavor with
vanilla and nutmeg.

Sallie Rogers McSpadden
(Sister of Will Rogers)
Chelsea, Oklahoma

Will lived with his sister Sallie and her husband Tom McSpadden when he
went to the Drumgoole School.

Old-Fashioned Sugar Cookies

2-3/4 Cups sifted flour
2 teaspoons baking powder
1/2 teaspoon salt
1/2 Cup butter or shortening
1 Cup sugar
2 eggs, well beaten
1 teaspoon vanilla

Sift flour once, measure, add baking powder and salt, and sift again. Cream butter thoroughly, add sugar gradually, and cream together until light and fluffy. Add eggs and beat well. Add vanilla. Add flour and blend. Chill 10 to 15 minutes. Roll 1/8 inch thick on slightly floured board. Cut with large floured cutter, and sprinkle with sugar. Place on ungreased baking sheet and bake in hot oven (400 degrees) 10 to 12 minutes. Makes 2-1/2 dozen 3-1/2 inch cookies. For holidays, sprinkle with red or green sugar, colored candies, or decorate as desired.

Karen Sue Sapp
Docent—Will Rogers State Park

"Just flew in from Santa Barbara and found a real, legitimate use for my polo field. We landed on it."

Oldtime Cinnamon Jumbles

Mix thoroughly . . .
1/2 cup shortening
1 cup sugar
1 egg

Stir in . . .
3/4 cup buttermilk
1 tsp. vanilla

Sift together and stir in . . .
2 cups flour
1/2 tsp. soda
1/2 tsp. salt

Chill dough. Drop rounded teaspoonfuls about 2" apart on lightly greased baking sheet. Sprinkle with mixture of sugar and cinnamon (1/4 cup sugar and 1 tsp. cinnamon). Bake until set but not brown.
Tempeature: 400 degrees
Time: Bake 8 to 10 min.
Amount: About 4 dozen 2" cookies

Governor Scott M. Matheson
State of Utah

Carrot Pudding

1 cup grated carrots
1 cup grated potato
1 cup chopped suet
1 cup brown sugar
1-1/2 cups flour
1 tsp soda dissolved in hot water
2 tsp. cinnamon
1 tsp. salt
2 cups seedless raisins

Mix all ingredients together and put into greased molds—fill two thirds full and cover with waxed paper. Steam well for 2 hours. Serve with butter sauce.

BUTTER SAUCE
1 cup sugar
1 egg
1/2 cup butter
Juice and grated rind of one lemon
1 tsp. ground nutmeg
1 cup boiling water

Beat egg slightly with a fork, add other ingredients except water. Pour boiling water in slowly, stirring while you do so. Keep sauce hot but do not boil.

Governor Meldrim Thomson
State of New Hampshire

Centennial Luncheon Apple Crisp

4 c. sliced apples
1 tsp. cinnamon
1 tsp. salt
1/4 c water
Mix together the above ingredients.
3/4 c sifted flour
1 c sugar
1/3 c butter

Rub the three above ingredients together. Drop mixture over apples.
Bake. Serve warm with Whipped Cream. Use a buttered 10x6x2"
Baking Dish.
Temperature - 350 degrees
Time - 40 minutes
Amount - 6 servings

Betty Blake Rogers, Will's wife

"The day I roped Betty, I did the star performance of my life."

Nutty Fudge Pie

3/4 c. pecans
2 T. cooking oil
Roast pecans 350 degrees for 15-30 minutes. Toss now and then. Drain on paper towel. Salt.

Fudge Sauce:
1 c. chocolate chips
1 c. small marshmallows
1 c. Pet milk
Salt

Cook over medium heat until thick. Stir to prevent sticking. Cool. Line pie tin and sides with vanilla wafers. Fill half of tin with vanilla ice cream. Pour 1/2 fudge sauce over ice cream. Fill with ice cream and press into pan. Top with remaining fudge sauce. Sprinkle top with pecans. Freeze. Serves 8.

Gov. Robert D. Ray
Iowa

Coffee Ice Cream

Serves 8
6 egg yolks, beaten
3/4 cup sugar
4-1/2 pints whipping cram
4 tablespoons instant Sanka coffee
1 tablespoon Vanilla extract
1/2 cup Cognac

Combine whipping cream, sugar, coffee and vanilla. Heat until it begins to simmer and then pour over egg yolks. Stir well and strain. Allow mixture to chill, stirring from time to time, until completely cold. Add cognac.

This recipe is one that was enjoyed by Mr. and Mrs. Louis B. Mayer, and was given by their daughter, Mrs. William Goetz.

Chocolate Nut Bars

2/3 c. shortening
1 pkg. brown sugar
3 eggs
1 t. vanilla
2 c. flour
1 t. baking powder
1/2 T. salt
1 c. walnuts
1-7 oz. pkg. chocolate chips

Cream shortening, sugar, eggs, and vanilla. Add sifted dry ingredients, nuts and chocolate chips. Pour into a well-greased 10-1/2 x 15-1/2" pan or a pizza pan with a 14" diameter.
Bake at 350 for 25 minutes.

Gail and David Sears
District Interpretive Specialist
State of California

Strawberry Roll Supreme

6 eggs, separated
1/4 teaspoon cream of tartar
1 cup granulated sugar
1 teaspon grated lemon rind
2 tablespoons lemon juice
1/4 teaspoon salt
1 cup sifted cake flour
2 cups heavy cream
2 tablespoons sugar
1/2 teaspoon vanilla
2-1/2 cups strawberries
2 tablespoons sugar

Beat egg whites until foamy. Add cream of tartar, beating until stiff. Gradually (1 tablespoon at a time) beat in 1/2 cup of sugar. Beat egg yolks until thick and lemon-colored. Beat 1/2 cup of sugar, lemon rind, and lemon juice. Gently fold egg-yolk mixture into egg white mixture. Sift flour with salt. Fold into egg mixture, gradually. Pour into foil-lined pan (15x10x1). Bake in pre-heated oven (375 degrees) for 18 to 20 minutes. When baked, turn out on towel that has been sprinkled with confectioners sugar. Remove foil from cake immediately. Roll up cake in the towel from the 10 inch end and let stand until cold.

Whip heavy cream adding 2 tablespoons sugar and vanilla.

Sprinkle sliced strawberries with 2 tablespoons sugar and allow to stand about five minutes. Reserve several perfect strawberries, slicing in half, to garnish top of cake roll.

Unroll cake carefully and spread with half cup of whipped cream and sugared strawberries. Roll the cake and frost with remaining whipped cream. Garnish with the halved strawberries.

Robert K. Dornan
Congressman—27th District
California

257

Banana Split Cake

1 stick margarine
1/2 cup sugar
2 cups graham cracker crumbs

Mix and press into 13" x 9" pyrex dish.
2 sticks margarine
2 eggs
2 cups confectioners sugar

Mix in electric mixer for 15 minutes, yes, 15 minutes. Pour over crumb mixture. Drain large can of pineapple chunks and layer over margarine, sugar and egg mixture. Slice enough bananas to make a generous layer over pineapple chunks. Cover with large container of Cool-Whip frozen dessert topping. Garnish with cherries and pecans and chill overnight. (Several hours will be satisfactory, if it is not possible to chill overnight.) Serves 9 to 12, depending on size of servings.

Cliff French
Governor, Mississippi

Pistachio Pie

Combine in small mixing bowl
2/3 cup sugar
1/4 cup water
1 unbeaten egg white
9 drops green food coloring
1 teaspoon lemon juice
1 teaspoon almond extract

Beat with electric mixer at highest speed until soft peaks form when beaters are raised, 3 to 5 minutes.

Beat 1 cup whipping cream until thick. Fold into egg white mixture by hand or with mixer at lowest speed, fold in 1/2 cup pistachio nuts.

Spoon into baked shell.

Sprinkle with crumbs.

Freeze until firm, 4 to 6 hours; cover.

James R. Thompson
Governor, Illinois

Dark Mocha Cake

5 oz. bitter chocolate, cubed
1/2 cup milk
1 cup sugar
1 egg yolk
1/2 tsp. salt
1/4 cup water
1/2 cup milk
1 tsp. vanilla
3 egg whites
1/2 cup butter
1 cup light brown sugar
2 egg yolks
2 cups cake flour
1 tsp. baking soda

In saucepan combine bitter chocolate and 1/2 cup milk. Stir over low heat until chocolate is melted and mixture is smooth. Stir in the one cup of sugar and one egg yolk. Cook, stirring constantly, for three minutes, or until custard is thick and smooth. Cool.

Cream the 1/2 cup butter until soft. Gradually add light brown sugar; cream together until mixture is light and smooth. Beat in two egg yolks, one at a time.
Sift and measure cake flour. Resift with baking soda and salt. Add to butter mixture in three parts, alternately with the water, remaining 1/2 cup milk and teaspoon of vanilla. Stir in custard.

Beat egg whites until stiff, but not dry and fold into cake batter. Divide batter into two buttered nine-inch layer cake pans and bake in a pre-heated 375 degree oven for 25-30 minutes, or until layers test done.

Turn cakes out onto racks to cool, then put together with French coffee icing. Frost top lavishly, or frost top and sides smoothly with remaining icing.

FRENCH COFFEE ICING

1 cup butter
1/4 teaspoon salt
2 Tbls. instant coffee
1 tsp. rum
4 Tbls. boiling water
2-1/2 cups unsifted confectioners sugar

Beat butter until soft; add salt and the instant coffee which has been dissolved in the boiling water.

Gradually add unsifted confectioners sugar. Beat for two minutes. Add rum and allow to stand for five minutes, then beat again.

Gov. Lamar Alexander
Tennessee

Sour Cream Cake

1 cup sour cream
1 cup sugar
Cream together well
Add
2 eggs, beaten
1 tsp. soda in water
1/2 Tbs. cocoa
1-1/4 cup flour
1 tsp. vanilla

Combine all ingredients and put in 9x11x2 lightly greased pan. Bake 350 degrees 25 minutes or until done to test.

This is David Janssen's favorite cake.

Berniece Janssen
Ziegfeld Girl

"There are two types of men in the world that I feel sincerely sorry for. One is the fellow that thinks he knows women and the other is the one t'iat is always saying "I know the Mississippi River."

English Toffee

Place 1 lb. butter in a heavy pan and melt. Remove 2 T and grease a jelly roll pan with it well, sides and bottom. Add to what is still in the sauce pan 2 cups white sugar, 2 T karo, 5 or 6 T water. Boil stirring very occasionally until it looks like thick greasy gravy with brown streaking coming up from the bottom when a spoon is pulled through it. It must catch at the bottom to have the flavor. Be careful; it burns fast.

While it is cooking, cover the greased jelly roll pan with large pieces of pecans, about 1 cup nuts. Grind fine 1-1/2 cups of walnuts, and have ready about 10 oz. chocolate chips.

When candy is cooked pour it slowly over the nuts in the pan. Let stand a minute or two, then pour half the chocolate on it. Let it melt. Spread with a spoon. Sprinkle with half the chopped nuts. Press in slightly with spatula.

To remove candy from pan, cover with a piece of foil which is turned under one end of the pan. Wrap the foil over the other end then turn the pan over. Repeat with chocolate and nuts process.

Let cool before breaking up.

About a pound of nuts is needed for this recipe.

Our very own in resident "Young Will." He portrays Will Rogers on many occasions and bears a resemblance to Will.

Wes Howard
Ranger, Will Rogers State Park

Pumpkin Cookies

4 c flour
1-1/2 c sugar
2 t baking powder
2 t soda
2 t cinnamon
1-1/2 c shortening
1 can pumpkin or 2 cups fresh
2 eggs
2 t vanilla
1 c nuts

Combine flour, sugar, baking powder, soda, and cinnamon. Mix until color is uniform. Add shortening, pumpkin, eggs, and vanilla.

Beat 2 minutes until blended. Stir in nuts. Drop by teaspoon onto a cookie sheet. Bake at 350 for 12-15 minutes. Cool, then frost.

FROSTING
5/8 pkg. powdered sugar
2 T sugar
5 oz. cream cheese, at room temperature

Wes and Donna Howard
Ranger, Will Rogers State Park

"The last few days I have read various addresses made on Lincoln's birthday. Every politician always talks about him, but none of them ever imitate him."

Strawberries and Custard Sauce

Wash and hull 2 quarts of berries and drain. Put in bowl and chill. Pour off any water and spread 2 cups strawberry jam thinned with 1/4 cup Kirsch over berries and serve with custard sauce.

CUSTARD SAUCE
In the top of double boiler, scald 1 cup heavy cream and stir in 2 tbsp. sugar. Beat 4 egg whites with another cup of heavy cream and warm this mixture with a little of the hot cream. Stir well and gradually add all of this to hot cream. Set pan over boiling water and cook custard—stirring constantly—until thick. Stir in 1 tsp. vanilla. Pour into glass jar, cover and chill. (This custard sauce will keep for a long time in the refrigerator, and is delicious over other types of berries, too.)

Pierre du Pont
Governor of Delaware

Strawberry Shortcake

2 Angel Food cakes
3 8 oz. containers frozen strawberries
2 pints of whipping cream
4 T. sugar

Tear or cut angel food cake into bite size pieces and place a layer in a 13" x 9" pyrex dish. Defrost strawberries and place in blender until well blended. Whip cream until light and fluffy, gradually adding sugar. Pour half of strawberry mixture over angel food cake, press down with a fork and cover with half of whipped cream. Repeat three layers once more. garnish with whole strawberries, if possible. Serves about 8.

If you are ever in the State of Mississippi, please come by and visit with us here at the Governor's Mansion.

Cliff Finch
Governor, Mississippi

Cheese Cake Cookies

1/3 cup melted oleo
1/3 cup brown sugar
1 cup flour
1/4 cup sugar
1 egg
1 tsp. lemon juice
1/2 cup fine chopped pecans
1 Tblsp. milk
1 eight oz. pkg. cream cheese
1 Tblsp. vanilla

Mix brown sugar, nuts, and flour. Stir in melted butter, mix till light and crumbly. Remove 1 cup for topping. Place rest in an 8 inch square pan and press firmly. Bake 350 degrees—12 to 15 min.

Beat cream cheese and granulated sugar until smooth and creamy. Beat in egg, lemon juice, milk and vanilla. Pour over baked crust and top with reserve topping. Bake 350 degrees about 25 minutes. Will freeze.

Mr. Bob McMillin
1979 President
P.A.P.A.
(Palisades Americanism Parade
Association)
1975—Citizen of the Year
Pacific Palisades

INDEX